# PHENOMENAL
# MARKETING SYSTEMS

# PHENOMENAL MARKETING SYSTEMS

## THE 14

### Fastest Ways to the CA$H in Any Business

# HOWARD PARTRIDGE

Sound Wisdom

P.O. Box 310

Shippensburg, PA 17257-0310

For more information on foreign distribution, call 717-530-2122.

Reach us on the Internet: www.soundwisdom.com.

ISBN 13 TP: 978-0-7684-0779-2

ISBN 13 eBook: 978-0-7684-0780-8

For Worldwide Distribution, Printed in the U.S.A.

1 2 3 4 5 6 7 8 / 19 18 17 16 15

# DEDICATION

This book is dedicated to Tom Ziglar, CEO of Ziglar, Inc., and the "proud son" of American legend Zig Ziglar.

If not for Tom (and his family) selecting me to be the exclusive small business coach for Ziglar's small business customers, I would not have been able to see my systems work in so many different businesses around the world in such a short time.

The experience of working with hundreds of business owners around the world has been invaluable, and our friendship is even more meaningful than that.

I'm continually blessed by your wisdom and faithfulness.

Thank you in advance for the legacy *you* are leaving all of us.

# Acknowledgments

I would like to thank all of the members of our business coaching program, The Howard Partridge/Ziglar Inner Circle.

It is your implementation of the marketing systems in this book that has proven the value of these simple strategies.

Your record sales and profits are proof that they work.

I wouldn't be the person I am today without the Inner Circle community, and this book certainly wouldn't carry the weight it does without you.

Thank you. I love each one of you.

# CONTENTS

# PHENOMENAL MARKETING SYSTEMS

My second published book, *The 5 Secrets of a Phenomenal Business*, featured a chapter called "Phenomenal Marketing Systems," which are the systems I used to transform my business from operating out of the trunk of my car into a multimillion-dollar turnkey operation, and the systems that are helping small business owners around the world to achieve record sales and profits. My companies still use these systems today.

There are three reasons I am starting this book off with a chapter from my previous book:

1. **This Is the Foundation.** In order to understand *The 14 Fastest Ways to the Cash in ANY Business*, you must understand my marketing systems, which were taught in *The 5 Secrets of a Phenomenal Business.*

2.  **New Experiences.** The final edits of *The 5 Secrets* book were completed in late 2013. Since then, I've taught these systems to companies across seventy different industries in our coaching membership alone, not to mention the thousands of business owners who have attended my workshops, keynotes, and conferences. Over the years, thousands of small business owners in hundreds of industries have applied these principles, and I've gained tremendous insight from the wide range of business owners who are using them—from doctors and CPAs to plumbers and carpet cleaners. From retail to wholesale, from authors and speakers, to coaches and consultants like me, all have helped me to see my own marketing systems in a new and exciting light. I've also figured out better ways to teach the concepts. Of course, you'll be the judge of that!

3.  **Go Deeper.** The *5 Secrets* book covered all five systems of a small business and their subsystems. This entire book is about marketing—more specifically, *what* Phenomenal Marketing Systems will *do* for you: get you to the cash fast!

You'll also find that some of the strategies are *sales* strategies, not marketing strategies. Together, they reveal the fastest ways to the cash in any business.

A phenomenal marketing *system* is a group of working parts that *duplicates results* consistently.

## Phenomenal Marketing Systems

What comes to mind when you think of the word *marketing*? For some, it's advertising or branding. Others might think of it as networking or "getting your name out there."

Of course marketing includes those things, but marketing is actually *everything* you do to *attract prospects* to your business. *Phenomenal* marketing delivers a meaningful *experience* that educates, engages, and entertains. A phenomenal marketing *system* is a group of working parts that *duplicates results* consistently.

What kind of results? Enough of your perfect target prospects to reach your sales goal consistently. A phenomenal marketing system consistently produces your perfect *target* prospect.

If you're attracting the wrong kind of prospect, your marketing isn't working. And if your sales are up and down because you don't consistently implement marketing, then you don't have a system. Too many business owners spend a lot of time and money "getting their name out there" but have no real system of consistently attracting prospects. Most often, a small business owner's marketing is a gamble more than a planned effort. Congratulations for reading this book. You now have the opportunity to be one of the few who escape that trap.

## CHAPTER 1

# THE ONLY THREE WAYS TO INCREASE SALES

Regardless of the type of marketing you do, it must *increase sales*. Of course, the sales process will determine whether the prospect will actually buy, but that also depends on the quality of the prospect you are attracting. When you attract the wrong kind of prospect (because your marketing isn't what it needs to be), it doesn't matter how good your sales process is. You may even close the sale, but you won't build the kind of business you want if you don't attract the right type of prospect. Regardless of the type of business you are in, there are only three ways to increase sales:

## 1. Increase Sales from Existing Clients

The first (and possibly the easiest) way to increase sales is to get your existing clients to use your services or buy your product more often or sell more services. This can have a dramatic effect on your income. By marketing to your existing client base alone, you could literally double your business. This is assuming that you have something compelling and valuable to offer your past and existing clients, patients, or members.

As you'll see, marketing to your past and existing clients is one of the most important marketing activities. In fact, *not* marketing to your past clients is what I call the biggest marketing mistake of all!

It is estimated that it costs an average of 500 percent more to gain a new client than to keep an existing one. Existing clients already know you. You already know them. They have already paid your price. They are the most likely to do business with you assuming that you have a repeatable service and other products to offer. Plus, they're your primary source for referrals. If you aren't in touch with them on a regular basis, you won't build repeat and referral business, which is key to a profitable company.

## 2. Increase Number of Clients

Speaking of referrals, the second way to increase sales is to get more customers, clients, patients, guests, or members. This is the one that people usually think of first. Most small business owners say that 85 percent of their business comes from repeat and referral business, yet they don't have a system in place to maintain and increase repeat and referral business.

Most small business owners say they build their business through "word of mouth," but they don't have a referral *system* in place. There are many ways to get more clients, but the best way is through referrals, and I'll show you how to put your word of mouth marketing into a phenomenal *system*.

*Work less. Make more.* Build your word of mouth marketing into a phenomenal *system.*

## 3. Increase Price

This is a powerful way to increase sales, but many small business owners are convinced their customers won't pay more for their service or product. They are convinced that there is a limit put on pricing due to the poor economy, etc.

I hope to change your mind on this, because when you increase your price, you can even lose a significant amount of sales volume and make the same profit doing less work. If you raise your price and you don't lose much or any sales volume, you are making more money while working less!

*Work less. Make more.*

That sounds good, doesn't it? It's not that you shouldn't work hard. The point is that if you're like most small business owners, you're working too hard for the little you are making!

Once you understand your cost of doing business, a simple calculation will show you how much sales volume you can lose before it digs into your profits.

Positioning yourself and your company differently—by creating a different, more compelling message and creating, marketing, and delivering a unique experience your target prospects crave—will allow you to continually increase your price.

The beauty is that you probably *won't* lose any sales volume! If you do lose any clients, it'll be the unprofitable ones you don't want anyway. And if you do this right, you'll quickly replace them with clients who are willing to pay a higher price because you will have developed a compelling experience they want to have.

And the best part is that as you continue to build your business at higher prices, the profits really add up.

## CHAPTER 2

# EXPERIENTIAL MARKETING

Speaking of creating and marketing an *experience*, I came across a term some years ago that explained what I was already doing in my marketing, and explained how I was able to get the highest prices.

The term *experiential marketing* is sort of an unusual, obscure term, but is key to getting the highest prices for your service. In his book *Experiential Marketing*, Bernd H. Schmitt states:

> Today, customers take functional features and benefits, product quality, and a positive brand image as a given. What they want is products, communications, and marketing campaigns that dazzle their senses, touch their hearts and stimulate their minds. They want products communications and campaigns that they can relate to and that they can incorporate into

their lifestyles. The want products, communications, and marketing campaigns to deliver an experience…

Notice that it says to deliver an experience in the *marketing campaign*. Business owners should create the most unique and powerful experience when we actually serve our clients, but what this is saying is that it is created in the *marketing* campaign. Interesting.

The quote goes on to say:

> The degree to which a company is able to deliver a desirable customer experience (in the marketing) and to use information technology, brands, and integrated communications and entertainment to do so, will largely determine its success in the global marketplace of the new millennium.

You may not be concerned about the "global marketplace" in your industry, but the degree to which you understand and implement this concept determines the degree of success you'll have getting higher prices.

What is the marketing message of most business owners? How do average, everyday businesses advertise their services? If your industry is like most, you'll find that their message is either about *price* or about how they do their work. The features of the product or service.

Let's deal with price advertising first. Price advertising comes in many different ways. The most common type of price advertising is placing an ad that offers a low price. But that's not the only type. The way you carry yourself as a business owner is a reflection of the value of your service experience.

How you dress; what your company materials look like; how your company telephone is answered; and what your employees, your store, or equipment looks like will have a big impact on your perceived value. You see, you *will* take up a position in the marketplace, just by existing. The question is whether or not you will take up the position that you *want*. You have to *design* and create your position, rather than letting it happen by accident.

Jim Bardwell, who was one of my employees for eight years, worked with me as I was developing the marketing systems in this book. As I began to teach the systems to other business owners, Jim would sometimes teach some of the seminar sessions.

He always said, "You have to *assign* a higher value to yourself. You have a price tag on your head and your job is to assign a higher value by adding more value than the next person."

Every industry has a "going rate." That rate is on *your* head until *you* decide to change it.

## Avoiding the Three Types of "Price Advertising"

One of the worst things you can do in marketing is advertise *price* before *value* is proven. The most common type of price advertiser is the one that advertises a ridiculously low price with no intention of ever honoring that price. Or, they have one item in stock at that price. You can put this type of price advertiser in the "bait n' switch" category.

They bait the prospect with a low price to get in the door. Once the prospect is generated, the advertiser switches the prospect to what they really want to sell. In the worst case, the company would even refuse to offer the low price service. Let's say that you see an ad for a new car at a ridiculously low price. You arrive at the dealership only to realize they only had ONE vehicle at that price. (It was in the fine print.) Do you have bait n' switch operators in your industry?

The bait n' switch advertiser is only *one* of *three types of price advertisers*. The second type of price advertiser is what I call the *value* advertiser. Unlike the bait n' switch, the value advertiser is a legitimate business model, and has intentionally positioned itself as the lower price alternative.

Think of how Southwest Airlines started. They intentionally positioned themselves as the low price alternative and they were very focused about running their business model accordingly.

Not offering meals on their flights, their point-to-point routes, open seating, and the revolutionary "ten-minute turnaround" have all kept their costs low so they could offer a lower price and make a healthy profit. This model, however, doesn't work for the small business that doesn't have the scope or infrastructure that a larger company has.

This brings me to the third type of price advertiser: the "independent professional" (probably you). This is the small business that doesn't have the management infrastructure a larger company does. You don't have the market penetration a larger company has, and you don't do the volume a larger company does. You don't have capital they have and you don't have an advertising budget they have.

Let's think, for example, about a plumbing company. If a plumber has a smaller operation, why would he want to match the price of a bigger competitor?

He can't compete with their margins. He doesn't have the management infrastructure, the capital, the brand image, or the television commercials that the larger company might have. His revenue is generated by his sweat. Therefore, even though the overhead is lower, this person should charge more rather than less. The key is that this plumber must understand what differentiates him from the larger firm, which I will get to in a moment.

Let's look at a comparison between the smaller operator and the larger company. Let's say this is the income statement of the larger firm:

$5M Income

- $2.5M Cost of Sale

= $2.5M Gross Profit

- $2.0M Fixed Expense

=$500k Net Income

Compare this to a smaller operator. If a smaller operator who billed $200,000 has the same cost structure that produces a 10 percent margin, he would end up with $20,000 in profit. Not cool! And that's what is happening in small businesses around the world every day! Obviously, there are lots of variables in this scenario, but the point is that you can't compete with the larger company on price.

The bottom line is that price advertising attracts price shoppers. So, choose your pricing strategy to fit your business model and size.

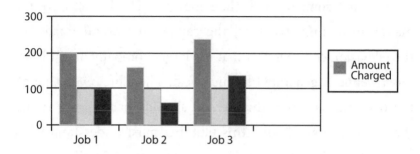

## The Effects of Lowering or Raising Price

In this simplified illustration, Job 1 (which could be Product 1) is priced at $200 and the cost of producing it is $100, which would give you a $100 profit.

Job 2 offers a discount of 20 percent, which would make the price $160. Guess what doesn't change? The cost! It still costs $100 to do that job! So that means your profit went down to $60.

That's a 40 percent drop!

What if you could position your company in a way that you could charge 20 percent *more* instead of less? What do you think would happen?

Let's take a look...

Job 3 is priced at $240 instead of $200. What stays the same? The cost! $240 minus $100 gives us $140 *profit*. And by the way, *the difference in profit from Job 2 and Job 3 is 2.33 times the amount.*

Or do the same volume and make more than twice the money. This is a very important concept for smaller companies to understand. With any company, it's not in the volume, it's in the profit. It is extremely important for independent business owners to understand this because they don't have a national brand to generate leads. Small businesses have an entirely different set of benefits to offer, which are worth far more.

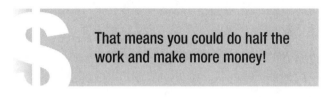

That means you could do half the work and make more money!

## How They Do Their Work

The second way that most small business owners advertise their company is *how they do their work*. Other than price, what could possibly be wrong with this? Let's look and see...

Let's say that Sue Smith is a CPA. When Sue introduces herself at a networking group, it will usually sound something like this: "Hi, I'm Sue Smith with 1-2-3 Accounting Firm and we do taxes. If you need anything to do with taxes, just give us a call. We do everything from soup to nuts, A-to-Z; you name it, we can do it. If you need anything, just gimme a call."

Isn't it true that just about every time you hear someone introduce their business, *nothing* stands out that makes them unique and different?

The problem is that everyone is saying the same thing. So why should people choose you over another company? Why should they pay you a higher price? They shouldn't. This huge mistake is repeated by small business owners every day. In today's competitive marketplace, it is not enough to just tell what you do or to tell the features and benefits of what you do.

## CHAPTER 3

# How to Dominate Your Market and Get Rich in the Niche!

**If you try to be everything to everyone,
you won't be anything to anyone!**

If you want to dominate a niche, you first have to know what your niche is. Do you know that when you try to be "everything" to everyone, you won't be "anything" to anyone? You want to be a *BIG FISH* in a small pond, rather than a minnow in a huge ocean. So, who is your perfect target niche client?

My good friend and business consultant Ellen Rohr explains a simple way to find out. Think about your very best customers. You know, the ones who never complain about price, they always pay on time, and they are a pleasure to work with. That picture describes your target niche market.

## Domination Is a Result of Positioning

In their classic marketing book *Positioning*, Jack Trout and Al Ries describe positioning as a slot in your target market's mind much like a file in a file cabinet. To illustrate this, let me ask you a couple of questions: when I say "laundry detergent," what brand first comes to mind? For most it's Tide. When I say "soft drink," what brand comes to mind first? Most would say Coke.

Whatever brand first came to your mind is the one that occupies the first folder in the file cabinet of your mind. So your job as a *phenomenal* marketer is to have a *system* for positioning yourself at the highest place in the mind of your perfect target market.

Positioning and domination is a result of creating, marketing, and delivering a UNIQUE EXPERIENCE.

Let's look at three companies that have done this well:

1. *Whole Foods*—they recognized the growing trend of natural food enthusiasts (target market) and decided to take up a position in that space.

2. *Starbucks*—They created a unique experience around coffee—a commodity that has been around for thousands of years.

3. *Harley-Davidson*—Whether you're a biker or not, you must agree that there's a unique experience

around owning and riding a hog! That could be good or bad, depending on your view!

## Delivering a Unique Experience Means You Can Charge More

Why do you need to charge more? Because working 24/7 just to barely scrape by is not a phenomenal life. Remember, the only reason your business exists is to help you achieve your life goals.

Why doesn't the *average* person shop at Whole Foods? Because of cost. I personally love to shop at Whole Foods because they offer the natural foods that I want. I pay more, but I get what I want all at the same place. My wife tells me I can get certain items cheaper at other places, but I'm not interested in going to three different stores to get what I need, and none of the other stores have the natural foods selection that I want.

## "How Much Can You Spend on a Cup of Coffee at Starbucks?"

Starbucks has earned the nickname "Fivebucks," because you can easily spend five dollars on a single cup of coffee. I decided to find how high I could go on a cup of coffee with Starbucks, so I conducted an informal marketing survey. As I traveled around the country, I would go into Starbucks, walk up to the counter, and say, "I want to buy your most expensive cup of coffee." Strangely, without any hesitation, they would point to the top of their board and offer something like a venti salted caramel macchiato or something like that. "How much is that?" I asked. "Six twenty-five," they responded.

"Can you make it more expensive?" I ask.

Your job as a *phenomenal* marketer is to have a *system* for positioning yourself at the highest place in the mind of your perfect target market.

"What do you mean?" they respond curiously.

"I want to buy the most expensive coffee I can."

Now they are looking at me very strangely.

"For example, could you add some shots?" I pressed.

"Sure."

"How many can you add?"

"As many as you want."

"Yeah, but the venti cup only holds a certain amount, right?"

"Right."

So, they figure that up.

Then almost without fail, another employee comes along and says, "You could add some flavors," and they begin to calculate all of the additions.

Then, they realize that the concoction isn't drinkable, or it has so many shots that it might be dangerous.

I assure them it's okay because I don't want to drink it, I just want to buy the most expensive cup of coffee I can find.

The highest price I have been able to find so far is $43.27!

Don't worry, I didn't pay it. In fact, each episode ends the same way, "Never mind, I'll just have a tall cappuccino." (They didn't think that was very funny, but I always give them a nice tip for playing along.)

I recently came across a video of a guy who did the same experiment with Starbucks. He created a great video of the interaction and the actual sales receipt!

Is Harley-Davidson concerned about being the cheapest bike around, or are they more concerned with creating the right experience around their brand? The company has created such an identity that people are willing to pay a very high price to own one of its products.

The brand is so strong that customers proudly wear its clothing and even get the logo tattooed on their bodies!

A couple of years ago, I held a leadership retreat in Colorado Springs, and a lovely couple in our coaching program rode their Harley all the way from Florida. They built a seventeen-day vacation around the event. I went outside to see their bike, and the husband was beaming as he showed it off.

As he uncovered the shiny motorcycle, with two seats and a trailer, I could immediately tell it was probably quite expensive. So, I asked, "Chris, how much you got in this bike?"

"Sixty-five grand," he responded.

"Sixty-five thousand dollars?" I exclaimed. "You know you can get a really nice car for that price, right?" I asked.

He immediately began justifying the expense with the model, type, the custom paint job, and so on. The real truth is that owning and riding the motorcycle is an experience that he wants. And he is willing to pay for it.

## The Experience Economy

To illustrate how this works, let me share a concept from a phenomenal book called *The Experience Economy* by B. Joseph Pine and James Gilmore. This illustration is about value offerings, and it happens to be about coffee.

When coffee first hits the market as a *commodity*, it costs about $1 per pound. There is not much differentiation at this point other than the type of bean. Once it is packaged and appears on the shelf at the grocery store, it becomes a *good*.

How much does a pound of coffee cost at the grocery store? Having presented this message thousands of times, I have found that very few people know how much they pay for a can of coffee! We just enter the store like zombies and grab our brand.

Coffee in the grocery store can range from $2.99 per pound (it's actually twelve ounces of coffee and four ounces of air—kind of like potato chips these days!), on up to more than ten bucks a pound. We have gone from *one* dollar a pound to *three to ten times the price!*

For what? Packaging. The brand.

How is *your* packaging? How is *your* brand? Most small business owners are at the forefront of their businesses. Did you know that the way you dress, the way you carry yourself, and the way you communicate *assigns* a value to you and your business?

The next level is the *service* level. If you go to Denny's and buy a cup of coffee, what are you really paying for? You're not really paying for coffee, right? You are paying for the *service* of someone brewing that coffee and making it available to you.

How much does a cup of coffee cost at Denny's? About one dollar per cup. How much of that *weak* coffee can you make from a pound of coffee? About sixty cups! So the price per pound goes up to about $60 a pound at Denny's.

When you think about your marketing message, are you talking enough about your unique service? When you sell the benefits of a unique service rather than just the work you do or the product features, you begin to set yourself apart and can therefore charge more than the commodity price.

## How to Get People to Stand in Line and Pay You the Highest Prices for Your Product or Service

Finally, the next level is the *experience*. This would be having a cappuccino in Italy outside one of the historical landmarks. My wife is Italian and we went to Italy for our twentieth anniversary. You aren't paying for coffee at that point; you're paying for the experience.

Another example of the experience level would be Starbucks. People stand in line to pay the highest prices for a cup of coffee—a commodity that has been around for thousands of years.

I have a picture I took in the Baltimore airport. There were sixty-three people standing in line at Starbucks. And that was just in a few minutes' time. There were hundreds of people who stood in that line to pay the highest price for a cup of coffee!

Now, here's a little disclaimer: there were two other coffee places in that wing of the airport that were closed at that time of the morning. Why were they closed? I can only assume that management felt there weren't enough outbound flights at that time to justify running the lights, and I can just hear them say that their employees don't like coming in that early anyway!

But Starbucks understands something the other coffee places don't. They understand that the people who stood in that line are going to walk onto an airplane with hundreds of other people on it. And they are going to have something very important in their hand—not just a cup of coffee, but the logo on the cup. The brand. That green siren will be tattooed on the forehead of each person sitting in the seats.

As each person sitting on that airplane sees that logo, it makes them wish they stood in line for it.

The question becomes "Can you do this in your small business?" And the answer is yes, you can. Here's how.

CHAPTER 4

# THE PHENOMENAL FIVE-POINT EXPERIENTIAL MARKETING MESSAGE

Several years ago I developed my Five-Point Experiential Marketing Message, which covers the five things that people will stand in line and pay the highest price for. When you have all five of them in place *and* you understand how to use them in your marketing, you can literally position yourself at the top of any industry.

I've done this myself in my own companies, and my systems have, at a minimum, helped thousands of small business owners around the world in many different industries improve their position, and many now dominate their respective markets.

Here are the five points:

1.   *Reputation.* There is one primary "unspoken" question that every prospect has about every person or

company they do business with. That question is: "Can I trust you?" Your prospects may not verbalize the question just like that, but it *is* the *number one* question in their mind. So in your marketing message, you must not only demonstrate *trust*, but *prove* that you have a phenomenal reputation. I will explain how to use each of these points shortly. The benefit of this point is that the prospect has peace of mind and is more likely to move forward with a favorable buying decision.

2. *Experience.* The second unspoken question all prospects have about your business is, "Do you know what you are doing?" I can trust you all I want, but if you don't have a clue what you are doing, what good is your business? Your marketing message must prove that you have experience in your field. The benefit of that to a prospect is that they will get what they paid for.

3. *Education.* The third point demonstrates that you are trained or that you have specialized knowledge. You can use this point to demonstrate that you are the education source, which has tremendous benefits to the consumer as well as to you.

4. *Systems.* This has to do with both the technical systems of your business as well as your customer service system. In other words, how will you service that client differently from anyone else? What

is different about your technical offerings? How do you do things differently from others?

5. *Guarantee.* The final point is to remove the risk of moving forward for the customer. Your guarantee, warranty, or stated commitment tells them that they don't have to worry about buyer's remorse. The way you structure your guarantee has great impact on your message.

## Two Versions of the Message

There are two ways you will use this message:

### 1. *In Marketing*

You can use this message to introduce yourself at a networking meeting. Remember the CPA example I shared earlier? She can use these five points to set herself apart and share the unique experience she provides. One can cover all five points very effectively in about sixty to ninety seconds. Some people call this an "Elevator Pitch."

Now, instead of using language that focuses on price or how you do your work, like everyone else does, you are "refocusing" your potential prospects on the five things that set you apart. By using the five points, you'll be able to convey a meaningful message in a short amount of time, which will set you apart and attract the best prospects for you.

Since the five points are the things that people will line up to pay a higher price for, every form of advertising or marketing you do should incorporate one or more of these points. This is done in various ways of course, and perhaps won't even use the same words I'm using in the five point message.

Everything you do in marketing will either build or diminish your reputation. Even a simple social media post. The post will either display your experience or reveal the lack thereof. Your post could be educational, therefore positioning yourself as an expert (a powerful form of marketing that we'll talk about in this book), or it could demonstrate your technical process or how you provided phenomenal customer service. Finally, it could showcase your commitment to following up after the sale.

Can you see how everything you do in marketing can communicate one of the five points?

## 2. *In Sales*

Once you've generated a prospect, your business may require a sales presentation. This may be done over the phone or in person. The benefit of doing a presentation is that you can discover your prospect's needs and customize your five-point message to fit their needs, concerns, and desires. (See *Phenomenal Sales Systems* in *The 5 Secrets of a Phenomenal Business.*)

If you have studied marketing at all, you may have heard of something called a Unique Selling Proposition (USP). A USP *proposes* doing business with you because of your uniqueness.

Experiential Marketing is so important today that I decided to call my Five-Point Experiential Marketing Message a UEP™ instead of a USP. That stands for a Unique Experience Proposition™. Describing the experience (rather than just the features and benefits) is critical today. People want to know what the unique experience they will have with your company will be.

## How to Use the Five Points

### Marketing Point #1: Reputation

Let's use Starbucks as our example. Starbucks gained a reputation of being the coffee experts. Whether they truly are or not makes no difference. People believe that they are and they buy the product in droves. Plus, the brand has become iconic throughout the world.

Starbucks did this in two ways. One, in the early days they raised some real concerns about how average, everyday commodity coffee is made. The worst stories revealed how imported coffees use dirt as filler! Through Education Marketing (a form of Experiential Marketing), they taught consumers how commodity coffees use an inferior bean called the Robusta bean. Starbucks uses only 100 percent Arabica beans.

Other coffee companies use conveyer-belt roasting processes, and of course Starbucks has its own special, patented roasting system. Commodity coffee companies use harsh chemicals during processing and have to use defoamer to smooth it out. Yuck!

Even though this part focuses on the product, the reaction is purely emotional (an experience), and questions the integrity of other coffees. Once coffee is ground up, how do you know what's in there? Starbucks then begins the process of educating you about its processes, which produce the *perfect cup*. Their main brochure started with the words *Experience the Perfect Cup*.

Marketing your reputation is done by using what others say about you rather than what you say about yourself! My friend Joseph Michelli, author of *The Starbucks Experience*, says, "A brand is nothing more than what people say about you when you are not around." The relationships you have with your clients—people with influence in your industry and community—will build your reputation and confirm that you can be trusted.

Testimonials are powerful ways to demonstrate trust, because what your clients and other important people say about you is more believable than what you say about yourself.

Celebrity endorsements are also another great means, if you can acquire them. If you have a local celebrity who recommends you, see if you can use that person's name in your marketing. For example, one of my companies was featured on a television show hosted by a local celebrity. Our phone rang constantly, and we soon learned that he had a radio program where he gave live endorsements in the ads. We generated millions of dollars in sales over the years just from that one source.

Successful high-profile projects or relationships with clients also help you develop your reputation (which translates into trust). Your involvement in community service speaks volumes. Awards and certifications are also great tools that build your reputation. Be sure to use all of these things in your marketing media.

What others say about you taps into a powerful human law called social proof. I was on the west side of Kauai, Hawaii, one day and the water was extremely rough. I noticed that other people were waiting to see if anyone drowned before they ventured in! This is social proof, which says if others are doing it, it must be okay.

Be sure to communicate how each and every one of these marketing points benefits the client. The benefit of reputation is obvious—the more you can trust a company, the more peace of mind you have in moving forward with them. An absence of trust means you would only do business with such a company if you had to.

Take every opportunity to build trust by building your reputation. Create, market, and deliver an experience that gives you a phenomenal reputation.

Here's an example of how reputation might be used when you are introducing yourself at a networking group:

"Our company enjoys a reputation that is second to none. Some of the area's most seasoned [experts in your area] refer our services/products exclusively."

### Marketing Point #2: Experience

There are two areas where communicating experience comes into play—one is how long you've been in business. "Since 1902" has an impact. "Over twenty years" is also a powerful statement. For example, I've owned my own business for over thirty years. That's three decades! I've been helping other small business owners with their businesses for almost twenty years of the thirty. If you want advice from someone, you want to know they've traveled the road.

The second area where experience comes into play is when your industry requires a certain amount of technical experience. You wouldn't want a heart surgeon who performed his first operation yesterday!

One of the ways our service company made tremendous progress with our positioning was by offering to tackle troubleshooting jobs that no one else wanted to touch. Anything that was weird or far out, I wanted to get a peek at it. This in turn gave us unmatched experience. We were going after things that others

**Take every opportunity to build trust by building your reputation. Create, market, and deliver an experience that gives you a phenomenal reputation.**

were running from. In just a few years, I saw more situations than my competitors will likely see in a lifetime. I was able to learn a tremendous amount from those experiences.

Introduction example of experience: "Our company has been in business for _____ years, and is experienced in all types of [whatever you do]. We will be familiar with your situation regardless of what it is…"

If you haven't been in business for very long, focus on the areas of experience you *do* have. You can also lean heavily on the next point.

### Marketing Point #3: Education (or Training)

If you are certified by your industry, you should educate your prospects and clients on what certification means. Certification can be a powerful marketing tool, but only if you share with your prospects how they can benefit from your expertise.

Talk about any specialized training or knowledge you or your staff has that can benefit them. And be sure to share that part of your mission is to educate them on how to navigate your industry. This sets you apart as a consultant.

For example: "Our company is certified by the [Your Certification Group]. We are heavily involved in our industry and stay on the cutting edge of information. We bring this education directly to you, so you can be sure you have the very best available."

### Marketing Point #4: Systems

This is how you will deliver your unique experience. Your customer service system will set you apart more than anything else. And the best part is that it doesn't cost much more (if anything) to provide a higher level of customer service. The key is to not just provide it, but to talk about how it is different and use it in your marketing message.

Usually, customer frustrations have to do with service, not necessarily the product. By identifying with the emotional distress of the typical customer, you can win many new clients. What are they suffering from? Identify the areas where your competitors are failing to serve, and promise to fill that gap. Be sure to explain exactly what you are going to do that is different.

For example: "Our mission is to provide you with the most phenomenal service experience ever. We will treat you with the utmost respect and courtesy and deliver your service/product on time."

In the sales version, you want to outline the steps you take that others don't.

For example, in a sales environment, you are able to spend time with a prospect asking questions. This is a luxury you don't have in marketing. As you interview the prospect about past experiences, you may find out that competitors don't deliver on time. You can outline how your company communicates through the delivery process.

### Marketing Point #5: Guarantee

Many small business owners are afraid to offer a guarantee on their product or service in their marketing message, but when I ask them what happens if their client isn't satisfied, they quickly point out how they make it right, including a refund if appropriate.

If you want to attract high-end clients, you must understand that they *expect* you to back up what you do. If there is any question about that, they will not move forward in using your services.

Using a guarantee in your marketing message confirms that you are the right company for them. If you are attracting price shoppers or people who just want to get something for free from you, you are attracting the wrong crowd. And that is not because you are offering a guarantee, it's because your marketing is reaching the wrong prospect.

Of course you are always going to have people who take advantage of your guarantee, so you factor that into your cost of doing business. If you can get more clients at higher prices because you offer a guarantee, you can actually make more money. Don't get emotional about people taking advantage of your guarantee. Instead, fund the returns with higher prices.

There are many industries that can't offer a money-back guarantee. If you're a homebuilder, for example, you can't give a refund on a house, but you can build a reputation that you follow up after the sale.

When my wife and I built our dream home in Houston, we had a wonderful builder who addressed every need that came up long after the home was built and signed off on.

That builder knows something that all business owners need to understand—how you handle your guarantee affects your reputation. So, you might imagine the five points being in a circle. Your guarantee is connected to your reputation.

Introduction example of guarantee: "Our company offers a 100 percent money-back guarantee. If you aren't completely thrilled with the service/product experience you receive from our company, we will rush back to your location at no charge and no obligation to correct the situation. If you are still unimpressed, you owe us nothing, and we will issue a 100 percent refund."

## CHAPTER 5

# THE FASTEST GROWTH TOOL ON THE PLANET!

If you want to grow your company really fast, you've got to get your message out to a lot of people, and quickly. One of the best ways to do it is what I call the "Free Trial Offer." This concept gives your prime target market the opportunity to experience your product or service before purchasing it. In the best case, it is an actual sample of the product or service.

For example, Chick-fil-A began to offer free samples in shopping malls. Now everyone does it. I met Dan Cathy, the CEO of Chick-fil-A, at the Ziglar offices, and he gave me his business card. On the back of it there was an offer for a free chicken sandwich.

The night before, Cathy received the Zig Ziglar Servant Leadership Award before a crowd of 2,000 people. He closed his acceptance speech with, "Come up and see me and get a card for a free chicken sandwich. And when you go to redeem it, bring somebody with you that will pay for theirs!"

This generated laughter of course, but think about this: here's the CEO of a multibillion-dollar corporation using the Free Trial Offer. He's not too good to promote his company, and you shouldn't be either.

I call the Free Trial Offer the *fastest growth tool on the planet* because I've learned that *the money is in the list.* Not just the size of the list, but the quality of the list—and the experience you provide for the list.

In the old days, you generated a prospect one at a time, made a presentation and closed the deal. There's nothing wrong with that, and you should continue to do that, but a better way to do this is to put a massive number of people on your list and allow them to experience some form of your product or service, even if it isn't an actual sample.

As I mentioned previously, my definition of marketing is everything you do to *attract prospects* to your business. *Phenomenal* marketing is creating an experience that engages, educates, and entertains. A phenomenal marketing *system* duplicates results consistently.

A Free Trial Offer system can do this for you. This system reaches out to *suspects* (people who fit the profile of your prime target market) and moves them to *prospects.* If someone is searching for a business in your industry, you can capture more prospects with a Free Trial Offer.

For example, if someone comes to your website and you don't have some way to get them to stop and provide contact information, you'll be at the mercy of only those who are ready to buy at that moment, and you'll be relying on other visitors to remember to come back to your site. By getting contact info via a free trial offer, you build a valuable contact list that you can now engage, educate, and entertain.

Another example is in-person. When you meet someone who seems interested in your product or service, you simply offer them the opportunity to either get on your list, or to go ahead and schedule their free trial.

Here's how it works:

You offer a free trial of some sort—it could be a free sample of your service or product, a free report, e-book, video, CD, audio book, a class, a consultation, or anything that will add value to your target prospects.

Your free trial offer allows them to "experience" your product or service, and/or to learn more about you and your offerings. At the time of this writing, I offer free business-building tips by e-mail, a free CD, and a free copy of my first book on audio.

Once someone subscribes to my e-mail newsletter, my company sends that person videos, webinar invitations, and ongoing tips and news. This helps my audience get to know me, like me, and trust me. I provide an experience by educating and entertaining my subscribers.

Those with whom my message resonates and who want to learn more will then move to the next level by getting my Home Study Course or attending an event, and eventually joining my coaching membership program.

Of course, not all do, but it gives prospects a way to learn about my expertise as I give them valuable information on how to build their business. By providing a free trial offer and getting a large number of interested people on a list, you're no longer begging individual suspects to try you out, you're communicating with a large number of people at once.

The money is in the list. Not just the quantity on the list, but the quality of those you invite to subscribe, and how you communicate with them.

I was coaching a marketing consultant a couple of years ago and asked him how many people were on his list. He had several thousand people on there from many speaking engagements. He offered an opt-in sheet at his presentations, which was smart. Even smarter, he diligently put them on the list.

Then came the big question. "How often do you communicate with your list?" I asked curiously. He sheepishly admitted that he hadn't communicated to the list in *months*! If he was phenomenally successful, that might be understandable, but he wasn't.

Did you know that even Lexus has a free trial offer? My wife and I have owned Lexus automobiles for many years. When I was considering my first new one, I was in the showroom looking at a specific model. Noticing that I wasn't 100 percent sure it was the car for me, the salesman encouraged me to take it home for the weekend. "I'm not sure I could get it back on Sunday," I replied.

"Don't worry, bring it back Monday," he insisted.

"Well, I'm driving to Austin Monday afternoon..." I continued.

"No problem! We'll fill it up with gas. Take it with you!"

What's happening here? Why would Lexus want to let someone take their car home without first paying for it? They want you to take that car home because they know that once you "experience" how it drives, you're going to want to keep it! And when you see how it looks in your driveway, you really fall in love with

*Phenomenal* marketing is creating an experience that engages, educates, and entertains. A phenomenal marketing *system* duplicates results consistently.

it. But the kicker is when your neighbor comes over and begins to *ooh* and *ahh* over it—there's no way that car is going back! Especially if you're a male! You know how that male ego is!

Zig Ziglar called that the "puppy dog" close. You bring a cute little puppy home and fall in love with it. That little dude ain't going back, for sure!

Make sure your free trial offer addresses the biggest pain point your prime target market has. My good friend and phenomenal marketer David Frey says, "Every industry has three top problems that are never solved." Find out what those problems are and offer the solutions. If your product or service fulfills a big desire, talk about that.

Make your free trial offer as informative and emotional as possible. This is a wonderful way for potential customers to experience your product or service in action.

Instead of trying to take someone from suspect (again, someone who may or may not be a good prospect) straight to a paying customer, the free trial offer takes him from suspect to prospect and allows you to do something very important—collect his contact information!

Now you're the one in control of the follow-up. Plus, the prospect has "raised his hand" for more information so to speak. He is telling you, "Hey, I'm a prospect! I'm interested!" All too often, prospects are skeptical and they want to check you out. The free trial is the perfect way for them to get to know, like, and trust you.

What if people take advantage of your free trial? What if you have a free trial offer and it costs you money to provide the free product or service, or if there is a cost in delivering or installing the product? This becomes part of your marketing budget. Most likely it will be less expensive than advertising and you'll get better returns. If you find that you have a lot of people who take advantage of your free trial but don't buy, you can change or discontinue the offer. But don't do that until you've checked to see how many *are* buying as a result.

Special note: Don't confuse the concept of the Free Trial Offer with a discount! A discount is a completely different concept. Using a discount to generate leads is attracting prospects based on price, and that is not what you want to do unless you are in the value market. When you attract prospects solely by price, you are already training them to discount your service, therefore assigning a lower value to the product or service.

**Special note: Don't confuse the concept of the Free Trial Offer with a discount!**

A discount or promotion is something you can do once they have already become a prospect. And if you like, you can do that immediately after they become a prospect. Special promotions or discounts are used as a tool to generate more business, but make sure you understand how much more you need to generate in order to make your desired profit. (Remember the raise and lower your price formula I shared earlier.)

There is certainly a time for special pricing, promotions, and discounts. I use them all the time—but only after I have established the value and I have generated the right prospect. And when you've done that, you probably won't need to offer a discount. Just create a sense of urgency in other ways (I'll discuss this further in "How to Create a Phenomenal Marketing Message," in Chapter 13).

## CHAPTER 6

# How to Generate an Unlimited Supply of the Highest-Paying Clients (Without Expensive Advertising)

Everyone agrees that word of mouth is the best advertising. Everyone knows the power in one person telling another about a service or a product. The problem is that casual referrals usually don't create a phenomenally successful business. To generate a massive number of referrals, you need a phenomenal Referral Marketing *system*.

I mentioned earlier that not marketing to your past clients was the biggest marketing mistake you can make. The second is what I call "chasing suspects." We've all been there. You meet someone who says he or she might be interested in your service or product. You spend a massive amount of time and energy chasing an individual and nothing ever comes from it. The person was a suspect, not really a prospect.

Instead of spending a lot of time pursuing an individual, let me show you how to generate an unlimited supply of ready to buy prospects...

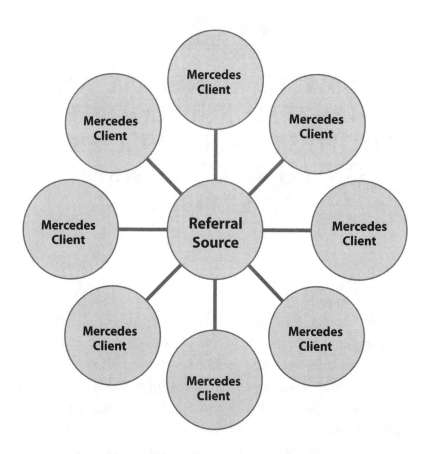

## The Secret to Record Sales and Profits

In coaching thousands of small business owners around the world, I've learned that most small business owners are missing out on a very big secret. This secret is how I have built my companies and how small businesses worldwide are having record sales and profits.

Here's the secret: Instead of chasing suspects and spending so much time following up with individual prospects, invest your time building relationships with powerful referral sources.

What I mean by a *referral source* is a company or professional that has a relationship with a large group of your perfect niche clients. For example, if you are a CPA and you get referrals from attorneys, invest your time building relationships with as many attorneys you can.

Here's an example: I'm the exclusive small business coaching company for Ziglar, Inc. They are a referral source for me. There are many small business owners (my niche) on their list. I'm also a referral source for Ziglar. Who needs Zig Ziglar products? Everyone! Especially small business owners!

Here's another example: Not too long after I began my training firm, Phenomenal Products, Inc., I approached a large supplier that had thousands of small business owner customers across the nation. We put together a joint venture; I traveled to their stores all over the country and they made sure the small business owners were there to learn from me.

We sold hundreds of thousands of dollars in business-building products and business coaching services, but what is most important is that it added value to them because they were helping their customers build their businesses. And it helped me in turn, as it was a phenomenal way for me to get in touch with a large number of business owners.

The first company I started is a business that cares for Oriental rugs, stone floors, and fine carpets for Houston's most prominent citizens including world leaders, celebrities, and athletes. Of course, we didn't start out with that clientele, but from the beginning, I grew the company by building relationships with flooring retailers, interior designers, and real estate agents. They refer their clients to us exclusively. That business brings in an average of two hundred new clients every thirty days just through referrals.

 My definition of Referral Marketing is: "The process of building a *network* of *sources* that will *refer* multiple clients to your business."

My first two books, *7 Secrets of a Phenomenal L.I.F.E.* and *The 5 Secrets of a Phenomenal Business*, were both Amazon #1 best-sellers in specific genres because I coordinated a launch with a dozen referral sources who promoted my books to their list.

My definition of Referral Marketing is: "The process of building a *network* of *sources* that will *refer* multiple clients to your business."

## The Top Ten Reasons Referral Marketing Is So Effective

1. *Your Network Is Unlimited.* As you begin to build relationships with powerful referral sources and you get your clients to refer you, the network continues to grow with no end in sight. The more you build and nurture those relationships, the more your business grows.

Casual referrals usually don't create a phenomenally successful business. To generate a massive number of referrals, you need a phenomenal Referral Marketing *system*.

2. *Higher-Quality Clients.* High-end clients will seek out a referral rather than responding to an ad with the best price. Being "referral based" helps you attract a higher-quality client. Referred clients usually don't even ask about price; they are more concerned about quality than price.

3. *Prequalified Clients.* By educating your referral sources, your prospective clients will be prequalified; therefore, they will already know more about you (and that you charge more than the commodity- or service-level company).

4. *People Trust Referrals.* Wouldn't you agree that referrals already have a level of trust in you? Sure they do. They trust you because the person they trust knows you.

5. *Reduces Competition.* With Referral Marketing, you are no longer fighting for the best ad placement or having your ads copied. Relationships are hard to duplicate.

6. *Low Cost.* With the right Referral Marketing system, you won't spend money on expensive advertising. The cost is very low for Referral Marketing. Even with a Referral Reward Program (which I highly recommend), the cost is still extremely low compared to most advertising.

7. High Returns. The returns can be huge. In many small businesses, a 4-to-1 return on investment on

advertising dollars would be outstanding. In other words, if you invested $1,000 in advertising, you would get an average of $4,000 in return. Most small business owners would be thrilled with that return. With Referral Marketing, if you pay a 10 percent referral reward and everyone cashed in on it, you would have a 10-to-1 return. In my reward program, I get a 20-to-1 return. (More on the Referral Reward Programs in a moment.)

8. *Returns Guaranteed.* With a referral reward, you don't pay until *after* the product or service is paid for. With paid advertising, you put your money on the line and hope for a return. Please don't misunderstand: there is nothing wrong with advertising if it works. More on that later as well.

9. *Small-Time Investment.* The biggest objection I get to Referral Marketing is "time." See "Exponential Multiplication!" below to overcome that challenge.

10. *Exponential Multiplication!* Would you be interested in how investing just a few minutes a day doing something really fun could potentially give you a return of more than $10,000 in new business each and every month after six months? Of course you would. Even though I can't guarantee it, I have seen it happen many times.

Here's what I discovered with Referral Marketing (see chart).

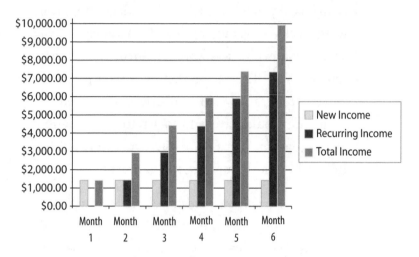

If you invested just thirty minutes per day calling on powerful referral sources (companies that are in a position to refer you on a regular basis), do you think it's possible to generate just $1,500 in new referrals in a one-month period? See the first column on the chart. Not too difficult for most small businesses.

What I discovered about Referral Marketing is that once you win the confidence of a referral source, they will continue the habit of referring you (New Income), unless you give them a reason not to. You will then continue to develop new referral sources each month, to the tune of $1,500 each month.

All told, at the end of six months, you would be at more than $10,000 per month in *new* referred business! The total monthly income in new business is demonstrated by the Recurring Income column.

This is how I built my first company from the trunk of my car to a multimillion-dollar enterprise. I still use Referral Marketing today. This is how I built a phenomenal training business and the reason you are holding this book in your hand right now. And it's the same method I have taught countless small business owners around the world. They are having record sales and profits because of it. Finally, it will work for you too, if you understand it and apply it.

You can clearly see why this strategy is the "secret" to record sales and profits. Yet, many small business owners still struggle to get out there and see referral sources. If that's you, hire someone! You cannot afford to continue to leave those dollars on the table!

## All of Business Is About Relationships

Would you agree that all of business and all of life is about relationships? You bet. So the idea here is to build relationships with potential referral sources. By adding value to them, they will add value to you.

Have you ever heard "It's not *what* you know, it's *who* you know"? Over the past thirty years in business, I have learned that *all* of business is about relationships. But, it's not just *who* you know, but it's *what you know* about who you know.

And it's not about who *you* know—but who knows *you* and *what* they know about you. That's called *positioning*. My good friend Bob Burg, best-selling author of *The Go-Giver*, says that people do business with those they know, like, and trust.

## Are You Building Phenomenal Relationships?

Are you actively building phenomenal relationships? Or are you just relying on casual word of mouth or advertising to get customers? How much time do you invest in business relationships? Or are you kind of stuck working "in" your business?

In today's digital world, we are more connected, but more isolated than ever before. I personally love social networking and actively network on Facebook, but I also make time to connect face-to-face, because nothing can replace that.

American legend Zig Ziglar said, "You can have everything in life you want, if you will just help enough other people get what they want."

Jesus said, "Give and it will be given back to you, pressed down, shaken together and running over." It may not come from the same person, but my experience has shown me that if you give people what they want, they will be more apt to give you want you want.

Jim Cathcart, best-selling author of *Relationship Selling*, says that "relationship selling is becoming an asset to others *before* they become an asset to you." So when you want to build a relationship with someone who can benefit your business, find out what they like, what they want, and what they need—and simply be the one to give it to them.

Best-selling author Jeffrey Gitomer says, "All things being equal, people would rather do business with a friend. All things being *not* so equal, people would still rather do business with a friend."

Again, Bob Burg says, "people do business with those they know, like and trust."

You see, you can have higher prices and a longer wait, but your referral sources will still support you because you are a trusted friend and advisor. While others are begging at the front door, trying to get by the gatekeeper, you are being graciously invited in through the back door.

If people don't know about you, they obviously can't use you or refer you. If they don't like you, they won't use you or refer you unless they absolutely have to. And if they don't trust you, they won't use you or refer you.

**All of business is about *relationships*.**

Finally, building relationships requires leadership on your part. My good friend John C. Maxwell (the world's number one leadership expert) says that leadership is influence. Nothing more, nothing less. We all have influence in other people's lives. How do you gain influence in someone else's life? By adding value to them. John says, "If you don't add value to others, you devalue them." Add value to them, and they will add value to you.

Remember, *all* of business is about *relationships*. You can know everything there is to know about the technical part of your business—and be *broke*! Not to say that being technically savvy isn't important. It is. But you can be the most technical person in the world and still be broke in business.

## The Value of Becoming a Phenomenal Networker

To build a phenomenal Referral Marketing system, you need to understand networking and how to build rapport quickly.

First, dress well. Did you know that people make eleven important assumptions about you in the first thirty seconds of meeting you? Most of this happens before you even open your mouth! First impressions last, so you want to make it a good one!

My personal view is that this is an area where many small business owners and professionals are failing. We have become so casual in our culture that we aren't even aware of the impact of dressing professionally. You influence others in how you dress and groom yourself. Positively or negatively.

My goal is to always be dressed sharp without overdoing it. If you are going to build powerful business relationships, you need to look like a businessperson. Wear a sport coat and a tie if you are a man. Wear a dress or nice pantsuit if you are a woman.

Make sure your clothing is professionally pressed, your shoes are shined, and your accessories are appropriate. Your hair should be well groomed, your fingernails clipped and clean; be clean shaven, and keep some breath mints with you at all times! No one likes spending time with someone whose breath could melt butter!

Always have business cards (or brochures) with you. Don't go *anywhere* without business cards! Keep a stack in your pocket, a stack in the car, and keep your extra supply wherever you keep your car keys. When you meet people, always get *their* card. It is much more important for you to get their cards, because there is no guarantee that they will call you, so be sure to follow up with them. Ask them for permission to add their names to your marketing list.

Be gracious. When you are in a networking environment, you are not there for you! You're not there to eat and take advantage of the food and drink. You are there to build relationships, so prefer others before yourself. Be polite and kind. Be positive and likeable.

Avoid getting into negative conversations. Sometimes you will run into people at networking groups who want to talk about the weather or complain about the food, or whatever. Keeping in mind that you are not there for you, avoid these conversations. They are not productive, and they bring everybody down.

Don't stand in the corner all alone. Instead, identify those who could be good referral sources for you and strike up a conversation. When you begin speaking with them, instead of being anxious to share what *you* do, show interest in what *they* do. Find out as much as you can about them and their business. This will come in handy when you get to talk about your business. People love nothing more than to talk about themselves and their business. In fact, a great exercise is to practice asking as many questions as possible without saying anything about yourself until they ask. Once they ask, that means they will listen closer to what you have to say.

Listen emphatically. Instead of halfway listening (called "selective listening"), listen closely to what the other person is saying. Use nods and positive affirmations to let them know you are interested in what they are saying.

Even if you aren't interested in what they are talking about, you should be—at least from the standpoint of how you will build a professional relationship with this person. Try to discover ways you can help them and add value to their business.

Remember why you are there: you are there to build your business. To build relationships, to find out how you can help others so they will in turn help you. You are not there for personal reasons. Keep your goals in mind and make the time investment worthwhile.

## Follow Up

Immediately put their name and address into a database. Every card you gather, immediately put the information into a database. If you are strapped for time, hire a high school or college student to do data entry for you. Then follow up immediately by sending the new contact a "Nice to Meet You" letter or card and an info packet. You should develop an information packet that shows why prospects should choose you over someone else.

You should have a follow-up system that includes an initial information package, regular mailers, and a regular e-mail newsletter. (More about this in Client-Based Marketing.)

Put them on your calendar to call the following week or whenever you told them you would call. The late Zig Ziglar said, "The fortune is in the follow-up." But also remember that your goal is to make so many contacts that you don't have to chase individual suspects to survive.

Download my free, step-by-step networking script, which is proven to build rapport. Just scan the QR Code or visit this link: http://www.howardpartridge.com/networking.

# CHAPTER 7

# THE SECRET WEAPON!

Once you have identified past referral sources, you now have a profile of potential referral sources. Now it's time to make a visit to their office or store. There is one secret strategy that will do more for your referral relationship program than anything else.

What is this powerful secret? Food. Yes, food. In particular, donuts, chocolates, pizza, lunch, candy, snacks, etc. Food is the international language that everyone understands! It's the one thing that can gain the attention that you cannot get any other way. The reason is that feeding someone taps deep into the Law of Reciprocity, which says, "If you give me something, I give you something." With food it goes deeper. It penetrates our most primitive makeup. If you feed me, I owe you the time of day. If you give me a treat, I owe you at least a couple minutes of time!

Remember the Five-Point Marketing Message from earlier? What a great time to share it—while they are partaking of the delicious brownies or candy you just brought! If you walk in with sales materials, what's their posture? Busy! Too busy to talk. But if you walk in the door with a box of Krispy Kreme donuts, they will listen to every word you have to say! It's amazing, and I have seen it work over and over again.

I first learned this from my wife, Denise. She's in radio sales, and I noticed that she would take goodies to her clients. For example, she would take cinnamon rolls to them in the morning and milk and cookies in the afternoon. She even had a company that made custom chocolate bars and she had the client's logo branded on the chocolate bar.

Just about every night she's wrapping gifts for clients and people in her network. All of the closets in our house are jammed with gifts that don't belong to anyone yet. She buys things as she sees them, then when there's a need, the wrapping begins! I finally "got it" one hot summer morning when she was walking out the door to go to work with a laundry basket full of things for the pool—squirt guns, goggles, and flip-flops. "Where ya goin' with that stuff?" I asked. "Oh, a lot of my clients have kids, so I'm bringing them stuff for the pool." *Hmmm...,* I thought to myself.

I decided to try it out.

There was a large potential referral source that I had called on eleven times (yes, *eleven* times). I had nice brochures and a nice introduction, but I didn't have the secret weapon. Every time I went into this place, I got the same response—a stiff arm came up along with, "We're real happy with the people we're using right now. Thanks for coming by." But this time I went to the grocery store and bought a little box of chocolates for $2.99.

I walked in and a lady down the hall noticed me come in. I introduced myself and she responded with the same stiff arm answer. She obviously didn't see the chocolates, so I said, "But I brought chocolates," with a little smile on my face. You should have seen her body language change! She went from the stiff arm pose to standing in front of me holding the box of chocolates almost close to her heart. I could almost hear her thinking, *Who is this nice man bringing me chocolates?!* Within seven days, we began getting referrals from that company. And they became a consistent referral source for us from that point on.

One of my early members increased his business $30,000 per month by making Friday "Donut Day." He and his wife loaded up the truck with branded boxes of donuts every week and set out to see as many referral sources and accounts as they could. I ran into him at a conference recently, and he told me it has continued to work so well that he now has other people delivering donuts on a regular basis. That is the case with us as well.

Another profitable "food" example comes from an auto repair shop called Freedom Automotive. My service company has a nice clean fleet of vehicles parked outside. Freedom Automotive obviously noticed the fleet, and one morning a box of donuts and a little card from Freedom Automotive showed up at our office. The next week, another box of donuts. After about the fourth or fifth week, I saw my operations director walking down the hall with a fistful of donuts and Freedom's card. He said, "We should at least give them a try." (I mean after all, they might stop sending us donuts if we don't, right?)

So we called Freedom, and they came to the office and gave us a presentation. They charged more than the shop we currently used. "Yeah, but the shop we use doesn't even say thank you. They don't care about us," we argued to ourselves. In Freedom's presentation, they showed us how following their maintenance plan would actually save us money. Who do you think we now use? Freedom Automotive. This took place about twenty years ago, and we still use them today. I know what you're wondering, *Do they still have donuts delivered?* Yes, they still have donuts delivered.

Find out what your major accounts and your referral sources like and take it to them. If they like Dove bars, take Dove bars to them. If they like Starbucks chocolate-covered espresso beans, bring those along with you when you visit.

## The $12,800 Chocolate Bar

Rick Jones, one of our coaches in my coaching company was with Dale Carnegie Institute for more than thirty-three years. He owned the Houston franchise for more than twenty of those years. My wife began to call on him to sell him radio advertising. The first time she called on him, she brought a huge custom chocolate bar with the institute's logo on it.

Certainly impressed, he kept the conversation open about radio advertising and eventually invested $12,800 in radio advertising the first time around. Over the years Rick became a dear friend and one of my most valued mentors, and our coaching clients love him. He jokingly says the candy bar cost him twelve grand. But the real message here is how a chocolate bar, coupled with phenomenal business relationship building, ended up in a very special life-changing relationship.

We have all of our existing and potential referral sources on a route. Every month we deliver cookies, pies, cakes, or whatever.

**The real message here is how a chocolate bar, coupled with phenomenal business relationship building, ended up in a very special life-changing relationship.**

We have a number of other "food strategies" too. For example, we cook breakfast for referral sources, hold referral appreciation lunches, and more.

What if your referral sources aren't local? I use a program called Send Out Cards. Send Out Cards will send a custom greeting card through the mail for you. Along with the card, you can send cookies, brownies, and many other gourmet food items. Their brownies are legendary! You will need a sponsor for Send Out Cards. Check with the person who gave you this book. If they are a distributor they can help you. If not, contact Phenomenal Products.

No matter what, Send Out Cards *must* be part of your relationship marketing process! I'll talk more about Send Out Cards later.

## CHAPTER 8

# WHO LIKES MONEY?

Have you noticed that most people like money? Zig Ziglar used to say, "Money isn't the most *important* thing in life, but it *is reasonably* close to oxygen!" To maximize your referrals, you should definitely offer a financial reward. You will get more referrals and your advertising dollars will go down. Sure, you can get referrals without a reward, but you will get many more if you offer a reward. Plus, offering a referral reward gives you something to talk about. If you don't offer a reward of some kind, it makes it harder to ask for referrals without appearing selfish. Remember, everyone listens to the same radio station: WIIFM (What's In It For Me).

A good Referral Reward Program offers anyone who refers a new client to you a reward in cash or products and services. Example: Suzy refers Bob, who is a new client. Bob spends $500 with you and your referral reward is 10 percent. You mail a Referral Reward Certificate to Suzy for $50. She can then redeem that certificate for products or services or she can cash it in. It's best to give the customer a choice. It can be a flat fee instead of a percentage of sale if you like, but make it significant.

Now, Suzy receives this wonderful Referral Reward Certificate and she can decide whether she wants to redeem it, throw it away, or give it to someone else. Here's where it gets interesting. The certificate is just like cash and can be given to a favorite charity, a friend, or whatever the person wants to do with it. Suzy doesn't want to take money from you and doesn't need your service or product right now, but she has another friend who does.

Remember, everyone listens to the same radio station: WIIFM (What's In It For Me).

Suzy refers Cathy. Cathy calls you up or walks into your store and says, "Can I use this certificate?"

"You bet!" you say.

Cathy spends $500 with you and you take $50 off (the value of the certificate). Her bill is now $450. She is a new client referred by Suzy and Suzy will now get *another* certificate for $45 for referring Cathy. Does Suzy have more friends?

You bet she does!

At this point, you are probably thinking, *Boy, that sounds like a lot of money to give away.* Let me ask you this question: Do you know what it costs you to gain a new client? For example, if you invest $1,000 in advertising, would you be happy with a $4,000 initial return? If so, that just cost you *25 percent* to gain that new client, compared to *10 percent* in this example.

"But, Howard, I already get referrals," you might say. My experience of implementing this with business owners around the world is that you'll get more referrals by offering a reward. And, by the way, don't people deserve a reward for going out of their way to support your business?

My experience is that most small businesses will have fewer than 50 percent of the certificates cashed in. For one reason or another, they never redeem them. That means a 10 percent referral reward is now costing you only *5 percent*! Also, be sure to put an expiration date on the certificate. We use a one-year expiration.

How much should you offer? Determine what your new client acquisition cost is and go from there. If you are spending money on direct advertising, what is your best return? Use that as a guide. What return would you be happy with?

We offer 10 percent in my service company. Anyone who refers a new client gets a referral certificate for 10 percent of the first job. After that, they are a repeat client. Fewer than half of the certificates are ever redeemed, so I am spending only 5 percent to gain a new client (that's a 20-to-1 return, by the way). What's more impressive is that the referral rewards we actually pay out are less than 1 percent of our total revenue.

Phenomenal Products currently offers a $300 reward for a new coaching client, and we even have a certification program where members can become referral partners and make 10 to 35 percent, depending on their level.

To maximize your referrals, you should
definitely offer a financial reward.
You will get more referrals and your
advertising dollars will go down.

You can offer a percentage or a flat fee, but you must make sure it is attractive enough for people to take the extra step to refer you. Is everyone motivated by money? No. Can everyone accept a reward? No. Some industries have rules against referral rewards or commissions. Therefore, we put on our certificate: "If you have a conflict of interest or cannot accept this reward, please pass this on to a client or someone else."

Promote your Referral Reward Program to your clients and potential referral sources as often as possible. We promote our Referral Reward Program by saying, "Get Free CASH or FREE SERVICE with Our Referral Reward Program!"

Every time a new customer buys from us, we have a system of recording how they were referred (online and offline). They are tagged as being referred by that person. Then we have a process of sending referral certificates or affiliate funds to that person. It's as simple as that.[1]

I'm sure you have more questions about a Referral Reward Program, but my challenge is that I don't have enough space and time in this book to teach you the ins and outs of a proper referral reward program. Also, getting the details right will be the difference of it working or not, so scan the following QR code to see how you can get our training program on how to create your own Referral Reward Program for your business.

One final note: If you offer a referral reward, be sure to honor it and pay it promptly! The worst thing you can do is promote a referral reward and fail to pay it.

---

1  If you are not one of our coaching clients yet, please change this significantly to protect the interest of our members. Thank you for your integrity.

To get a Free Report on how my Referral Reward Program works, scan the QR Code or go to www.howardpartridge.com/referralreward.

## CHAPTER 9

# ADVANCED REFERRAL MARKETING STRATEGIES

Once you build a solid relationship with referral sources and you are giving them the top three things they cherish (support, food, and money!), you can take it to the next level with these advanced strategies:

*Cook Breakfast or Lunch:* We have a system in place where we go to a client's site and cook bacon and eggs, fajitas, etc., for our referral sources. One of my clients built a really cool trailer with a grill on it. They do fajitas and barbeque for their referral sources.

*The Free Lunch Program:* Hold a Referral Appreciation Luncheon at a top restaurant. Invite past, existing, and potential referral sources to thank them for their support. We give out prizes, present a short talk, and even record video testimonials.

*Group Marketing:* The power of event marketing is that you are getting groups of referral sources together, which saves you a ton of time and also positions you as the expert. Events create memorable experiences as well. It creates a sense of community. Set up a Q&A or an educational talk for your referral sources, hold educational events (even get them approved for continuing education credits) or webinars. This positions you as the expert. Even if you bring in a speaker, you are the one who is making the experience possible.

*Golf Tournaments and Charity Events:* Get involved in events that your referral sources are involved in. Serve and support them and, hopefully, get the microphone!

*Joint Mailers:* Your referral sources send your phenomenal information to their clients to add value to them. This generates even more referrals as you are targeting a niche audience that has a relationship with the referral source.

As you can see, there are many Referral Marketing strategies you can use. And my experience is that Referral Marketing is the key to creating record sales and profits serving the niche clients you want to serve.

**Get your referral sources to send your phenomenal information to their clients to add value to them. This generates even more referrals as you are targeting a niche audience that has a relationship with the referral source.**

## CHAPTER 10

# How to Double Your Business in the Next Twelve Months (Without Adding a Single Customer!)

Does your business rely on repeat business? Is your primary referral source past or existing customers? If your business relies on repeat and referral business and you aren't marketing to past and existing clients, you're committing the biggest marketing mistake of all.

The biggest marketing mistake of all is not marketing to your past customers, clients, guests, or patients! Statistics reveal that it costs *500 percent* more to gain a new client than to keep an existing one. Did you also know that without consistent marketing, many of your clients will forget about you and eventually end up using someone else? It's a hard fact to swallow, but it's true.

A few years ago I participated in a home show with some service industry associates. After surveying a good portion of the attending homeowners, we discovered that they could not remember the name of the service company they had recently used—even though they were thrilled with the work—even when the service had been just two weeks prior! The company did a good job, but will never be in that home again unless they correct this *huge* mistake.

**The biggest marketing mistake of all is not marketing to your past customers. It costs *500 percent* more to gain a new client than to keep an existing one.**

A multi-industry study by the Wharton School of Business at the University of Pennsylvania revealed that companies who increased their customer retention rate by a mere 5 to 11 percentage points actually increased their profits by an astounding 25 to 75 percent, depending on the industry!

It is my experience that you could potentially *double* your business in the next twelve months without actually adding a single customer. In 1999, I proved how powerful this concept can be. One of my companies was mailing quarterly. We increased the frequency to twelve mailers. Eight additional months of mailing to past clients over a one-year period cost about $16,000 in printing and postage, but the return was more than $200,000 in trackable additional business!

Are you tracking your repeat business? Are you tracking your referrals? Are you tracking the returns on your advertising dollars? If you aren't, I can guarantee you are leaving money on the table.

## A Sad Story

When I started my first business, I worked in an upscale restaurant as a waiter. My wife and I were engaged there and celebrated many anniversaries there. The owners of the restaurant died and two sisters who worked there took over the restaurant. They weren't very good marketers and business became very slow. Every time we saw them they complained about how bad business was. My wife and I made suggestions, but they didn't seem very interested.

We knew they weren't doing many of the basic things they should be doing to get business. One night, as we were talking with one of the ladies, she was labeling postcards. Real nice postcards. I remembered them from when I worked there. Gesturing toward the postcard, I asked, "How well do those postcards pull?"

"Oh, phenomenal!" she said. "Every time we send them out we get tons of business. People come in and buy dinner and wine and sometimes they even bring friends with them." This was the first positive thing I had heard her say in three years! Then I asked,

"How often do you send them out?"

"About once a year," she replied.

I was shocked! Why do you think she didn't send them out more often? "Because it costs so much," she said. After being one of the top restaurants in Houston, Texas, for more than twenty-five years, that restaurant closed its doors. Out of business. Why? Bad food? No. Poor service? No. Just a lack of marketing knowledge. Sad.

Most small business owners don't understand the value of marketing to past clients. All they see is the cost. Then they want to go cheap and just mail to them or reach them by social media. Big mistake! A printed newsletter, postcard, or greeting card has much more staying power than an e-mail, which can easily be overlooked or deleted. Just yesterday I had one of my coaching clients tell me that sometimes my e-mails I send to her don't get read, but when I send a newsletter, she places it on the corner of her desk until it *does* get read!

And by the way, don't forget about the old-fashioned telephone! Simply pick up the phone and call past clients. This is one of the *14 Fastest Ways to the Cash*. Several scripts are provided later on.

To further irritate the problem, most small business owners don't know how to track their repeat business, which is completely different from tracking returns on paid advertising. With paid advertising, you invest a dollar and you track how many dollars you got back in new business. Many times when you market to your past clients, they may not respond to the offer, but they do remember you when they need you. Let me give you an example.

I was talking to a coaching client about this and he said, "My Client-Based Marketing isn't working."

"Okay, tell me what you are doing," I probed.

He told me that he was sending postcards with an offer, but no one was calling.

"No one?" I pressed. "No one" he confirmed.

"So, you're telling me that you didn't have *one single repeat client* over the past three months?"

"Well, of course I have," he said.

"Then why would you say your client mailers aren't working?"

I went on to explain that the way you measure the effectiveness of your Client-Based Marketing system is by tracking the *total* repeat customer dollars compared to the same period last year. Your goal is for that number to keep growing. It's the difference between a savings account with interest and day trading stocks. A savings account grows over time and collects interest. Your total balance continues to grow. Direct advertising is more like day trading. You make an investment and get an immediate return on it.

In Client-Based Marketing, you continuously invest a set dollar amount or a percentage of income, and you track all of your repeat business and all of the referrals that come from past clients (because those referrals probably wouldn't be there if you weren't consistently marketing to past clients).

Client-Based Marketing is more like a drip rather than a one-shot deal. Sure, you can have strong offers, but be careful with those because you don't want to train your clients to wait for a discount or special offer.

The goal is to stay in touch with them through engagement.

When marketing to your client base (mailing, calling, e-mailing), another hidden question to consider is, how much are you *losing* by not staying in touch? This is a hidden cost factor that is often overlooked.

Before even asking what the returns will be, consider what you are *losing*. You are losing valuable clients every day by not at least staying in touch. But for the sake of argument, let's say that you have one thousand clients and it costs you $750 per month to mail to them. That would be $9,000 per year. If you could add

$80,000 in revenue, don't you think it would be worth the investment? Even if it increased your business by only $36,000, it would be worth it. Plus, repeat clients are easier to service, they already know your prices, and you don't have to "sell" them. My experience has been that the long-term results will be more significant than that.

## Five Steps to Double Your Business (Without Adding One Customer)

1. *Get a higher price.* One of the reasons to constantly be in front of your past and existing clients (other than the fact that your competitor is marketing to them), is to reinforce your brand message that positions you at a higher value. Translation: higher price. Constantly remind them of the reasons to always use you and build the unique experience around your company.

2. *TOMA (Top of Mind Awareness).* Just because you did a great job doesn't mean your customers will remember you. I had $6,000 worth of plumbing done in my commercial building. I completely forgot about the plumber who had serviced my home on occasion. Why? Because he doesn't have a system to stay in touch. Do you? How many of your customers are gone because of not having a system in place?

3. *Sell more products and services.* You probably have a variety of products and services in addition to

Are you tracking your repeat business? Are you tracking your referrals? Are you tracking the returns on your advertising dollars? It is my experience that you could potentially double your business in the next twelve months without actually adding a single customer.

your main product or service. Marketing to your past clients can dramatically increase your income and profit margin!

4. *Increase frequency of use.* Getting your clients to purchase more often is another powerful thing that can add lots of dollars to your business.

5. *Referrals!* If your clients have trouble remembering your name, much less all the wonderful things that set you apart, what are the chances they are going to be able to refer you? No chance! A strong Client-Based Marketing program can dramatically increase your referrals, especially if you have a Referral Reward Program, and by teaching your clients how to refer you, will help them refer you to the right kind of clients.

## CHAPTER 11

# THE MOST PHENOMENAL MARKETING TOOL OF ALL TIME

Many of the country's top business trainers and marketers have recognized me as being a phenomenal marketer, so when I call something the most phenomenal marketing tool of *all time,* that's a BIG statement! This is a tool that I have been using, at the time of this writing, for more than five years. It's a tool that *any* small business owner or professional can use. And it's also a way that anyone can make money.

Now, before I reveal what this amazing tool is, let's remind ourselves that all of business is about relationships, and building your network of relationships is the most important business skill you can have. Building those relationships and staying in touch with your past clients are *the two most important marketing activities* you can be implementing.

Having said that, would you agree that one of the most meaningful tools you could use would be a heartfelt, personalized greeting card? This is probably one of the most valuable ways you can communicate to someone. Much better than e-mail and way better than a promotional advertising piece.

## But Here's the Problem...

To consistently write a personal greeting card to everyone in your network and on your client base list is nearly impossible. But what if there were a way to send meaningful greeting cards that not only touch the heart, but also position you as the consultant and remind your contacts to support you?

What if the business cards that you collected at a networking group weren't rotting away in a desk drawer, but were actually put into a system that was creating powerful relationships that can add great value to your life and career?

You can solve those problems with the most phenomenal marketing tool of all time! What is that tool? It's called Send Out Cards. Send Out Cards is a greeting card company where you can choose from thousands of greeting cards and they will mail the card for you in a white envelope that looks handwritten (incidentally, the reason that is important is people *always* open personal greeting cards or invitations).

Why do I call this the most phenomenal marketing tool of *all* time? Here's why: not only can you just jump on the website and send a card (through the US Postal System—it is *not* an e-card) it also looks personal and handwritten like an invitation and it has a real stamp.

You can even use your own handwriting and signature! You fill out a little form and send it to Send Out Cards, and they load your handwriting and signatures (you may have several, perhaps one from you and your spouse or business partner). Now, if your handwriting is as bad as mine, you might want to skip that option, but it gets better...

You can even create your own card quickly and easily and insert any picture that is on your computer. And remember, Send Out Cards sends that card through the mail in an envelope for as low as 93 cents plus postage (at the time of this writing). Send a card without a picture for as low as 62 cents plus postage.

Here are a few examples of how powerful this can be. Let's say you have a meeting with someone or you meet someone at a networking group. You take a picture with that person. Simply upload that picture and send him or her a card. Easy as that. I have a standard "Nice to Meet You" card template in Send Out Cards, so when I get a business card, I don't even have to create a card. My assistant simply selects that card and it is customized to the new person I have met.

Where can you get a full-color, custom piece in an envelope that you can have designed and mailed today for less than a dollar—in a quantity of one—in five minutes or less? The answer is *no place.*

When you collect business cards at a networking group, just have an assistant, a high school or college student (or even one of your children), enter the business card into the program and launch your "Nice to Meet You" card template that you've already designed.

Now, here's the interesting part, where it gets even better...

You can solve your problems with the most phenomenal marketing tool of all time! What is that tool? It's called Send Out Cards.

Not only can you create a card with any picture on your computer, you can send that same card to an entire group of people in your database. Each card is personalized to each person! How cool is that? Here are a few examples: let's say you have a small database of clients. Simply create a card and send it to the entire list. Your holiday and seasonal cards just became a breeze! Let's say you belong to a networking group that has thirty-five members. You take a picture at the meeting and send it out to the entire group. Or, you attended an event or went to a conference. You can send the group picture to each person and each card is personalized.

For example, my wife and I went on a group trip to the Tuscany region of Italy for our thirtieth wedding anniversary. My nephew, an accomplished artist and art teacher, led the group.

The group has bonded under the Tuscan sun with freshly made pasta, organic veggies from the castle garden, and the beauty all around. Each one of them will receive a lovely card with a group picture, photos of Tuscany, and some photos of their art. This is something they will treasure for many years to come.

It gets even better...

Phenomenal Relationship Marketing means remembering birthdays and anniversaries. Send Out Cards has an automatic reminder system for that.

Gets even better...

Along with the card, you can send chocolates, brownies, cookies, gift cards (like American Express, Starbucks, Home Depot), books, CDs, and many other gifts.

Gets even better!

You can create automatic multi-card campaigns. Earlier in the book I shared the importance of educating clients and staying in touch with them. A very important process is to "teach" new customers how to be great clients and how to refer you properly. So you have a series of cards that starts with a thank-you card. Next is a card that focuses on the referral program. Next a card that features one of your services, and so on.

Once you activate the multi-card campaign for a contact, Send Out Cards will automatically remember to send the card on a certain interval. If you think about it long enough you could activate a yearlong "Why I Like You" card campaign! Reason #1, Reason #2...

To use Send Out Cards, you will need a Sponsor ID. Contact whoever gave you this book to get their sponsor ID.

## CHAPTER 12

# THE PHENOMENAL POTENTIAL LIFETIME VALUE (PLV) OF A CLIENT

In his book *The Facts of Business Life*, my friend Bill McBean says a business owner's first responsibility is to protect its assets. Not just the assets on the balance sheet, but your client base as well.

My good friend and marketing master David Frey says, "The money is in the list!" Not just the number of people on the list, but the quality of the list and the quality of the relationships you've developed with them.

Have you ever thought about the value of your list? Have you ever thought about the *potential lifetime value* (PLV) of a single client? This exercise will astound you, and from this moment on you will have a greater appreciation for your clients. Far too often, a customer's value is judged by a single transaction rather than their long-term value. They bought a low-priced product or did a minimum job, so you're tempted not to market to them. Big mistake. They may have just been trying you out.

Many years ago, when I was first starting out in my first business (an in-home service company), I was the only employee and had no training in business. I quoted a very low minimum charge over the phone, assuming it was indeed a "minimum" job. Upon arriving, I realized I had totally underpriced myself for the project. Instead of making excuses, I smiled and went to work. After all, it wasn't the client's fault that I didn't have a good pricing system! Turns out the client was the facilities manager for the *largest* branch banking system in Texas at the time, which, the following day, became my biggest account. I made a *lot* of money from that bank for many years. Had I made excuses and judged her based on how much money she spent with me on that first project, I would have never gotten the big account.

Take a moment to jot down the average amount a single client invests with you each year. Now multiply that by twenty years. Example: Let's say a single client invests $2,000 per year with you. Twenty years x $2,000 = $40,000. Now, multiply that number by the number of referrals you could potentially get. Let's say it's just two per year. That's an additional $80,000 in potential lifetime value, giving you a total potential lifetime value of $120,000!

This is how you should look at the economic value of a client (while also remembering that they are human beings who should be treated well). Are you planning on being around for twenty years? By the time you get this book, I will have been in business for more than thirty years. Protect your assets. The most valuable asset is your client list. When you sell your business, the predictable income is probably going to be the biggest factor. And by the way, if you teach your team to value customers at this level, will it make a difference in how they see them? You bet it will.

## CHAPTER 13

# PHENOMENAL DIRECT ADVERTISING

Direct advertising is when you place an advertisement to reach your end user client. *Phenomenal* direct advertising is when you generate your perfect niche prospect. A phenomenal direct advertising *system* consistently duplicates results.

Although direct advertising can bring you phenomenal results in some industries if it is done right, this is not the area to "wing it." Direct adverting usually isn't cheap, and I've seen too many business owners literally go broke paying for ads that never had a prayer of working!

Here are some guidelines to help you have more success in any advertising you do…

1.   *What results do you want?* Anytime you are using paid advertising, be sure to understand what return on investment (ROI) is that you are

looking for. In other words, when you invest $1 in advertising, how many do you need to get in return? Many times you won't know this until testing the ad, which is the reason I do mostly relationship marketing. Direct advertising can be costly. On the other hand, I have used paid advertising for my companies that have generated huge returns.

2. *Who is your target audience?* The second thing to think about when advertising is who your audience is. At any given time, you may be placing advertising to reach:

   - A *Suspect* (someone who fits the demographic of your perfect niche market).

   - A *Prospect* (someone who has already expressed interest, but has not become a customer yet).

   - A *Customer or Client* (someone who has purchased before). In this case you want to generate repeat business, sell additional products and services, or to compel the customer or client to move to a higher-level membership, or something of that nature.

   Each of these audiences requires a different approach because of your *permission* level. The more they want to hear from you, and anticipate hearing from you, the higher the "permission" level.

*Permission Marketing* is a powerful concept (from the book *Permission Marketing* by Seth Godin) every marketer needs to understand to be more effective. You may need to have a process of moving suspects to prospects before they become a customer. For example, a suspect becomes a prospect by agreeing to get on your list and get more information. Your Free Trial Offer is a great example of moving people from suspect to prospect. Then you'll have a process of moving them from prospect to customer, then customer to client. You might have different names, like guest or member instead of customer or client, but you get the idea.

A customer is different from a client. An advocate or raving fan is someone who has moved beyond client status. You market to them differently.

3. *What do you want them to do?* When you are placing an ad or presenting a message to an audience, think about what action you want them to take as a result of the message. Start with the end in mind. Do you want them to call you? Do you want them to opt-in for something? Do you want them to visit a website? If you are speaking to a group, do you want them to come up to you afterward? Do you want them to fill out a form? Do you want them to buy something? If so, what? This is your *call to action*. We'll talk about that in a moment.

4.  *What message do you want to deliver?* What message is going to get them to take the action you want them to take?

## How to Create a Phenomenal Marketing Message

There are plenty of books and resources on writing copy, so I won't attempt to teach you everything you need to know about copywriting—or marketing, for that matter.

Plus, one book won't do the job, no matter how in-depth it is. The good news is that you don't have to be an expert copywriter to be successful in marketing your business, but understanding how to structure a message will help you in all areas of your marketing, whether it is addressing a group of referral sources or creating a brochure. But it is *vital* to the success of any direct advertising you do.

## Three Vital Components of Creating Phenomenal Marketing Copy

### 1. A Phenomenal Headline

Your headline is the first thing someone sees or hears in your ad. It would be the main heading in a print ad, or the first words spoken in an audio message. In a video or TV ad, it could be either or both. It has been said that the headline constitutes 80 percent of your ad's effectiveness. After all, if it doesn't even get noticed, what's it really worth?

Here are some tips to create a dynamic headline:

*Phenomenal* direct advertising is when you generate your perfect niche prospect. A phenomenal direct advertising *system* consistently duplicates results.

- The headline should draw your readers in. The headline should get their attention so they will be intrigued to read more. Some have called the headline "the ad for the ad."

- The headline should say as much as possible. In other words, the headline should give as much information as possible about the message that follows. Obviously you are limited, but keep crafting the headline until it says the precise thing that you want readers to know as if that's *all* you could tell them. Long headlines are a good way to accomplish this.

- Mention benefits. Readers are interested in what you can do for *them*. What is the benefit to *them*? Write what the service *does*, rather than what it is. Put benefits in your headline.

- Get emotional. Use emotionally charged words rather than technical- or feature-based words. See the following list of the thirteen most powerful words in advertising.

- Target only your audience. The more you can prequalify your prospects in advertising, the fewer unqualified calls you will generate. Use copy that will appeal to your target market only.

- Don't use tired clichés. Don't use worn-out, meaningless phrases. Clichés don't work, and they don't really mean anything significant.

**Headline samples:**

- Avoid Uneducated, Uninformed, and Sometimes Downright Unscrupulous <Insert Your Industry Type>!

- Avoid Uneducated, Uninformed, and Sometimes Downright Unscrupulous <Insert Your Industry Type>! *Instead, Get the Most Outstanding Service Experience Ever!*

- Avoid Uneducated, Uninformed, and Sometimes Downright Unscrupulous <Insert Your Industry Type>!

- How To Select A Professional <Insert Your Industry Type>

- *Don't choose a <Insert Your Industry Type> until you read this important information...*

- 5 Reasons You'll Love Our Service

- 7 Reasons to Call (Company Name) Before Calling Any Other Company

- 3 Reasons...

- 5 Reasons...

- 7 Reasons...

- 10 Reasons...

- 5 Ways to...

- How to Protect Yourself Against...

- Top 10 Reasons to... (do whatever you do) Now!

### 2. Phenomenal Body Copy

Your body copy is the core message that makes your case. Here are some principles for creating this part of your message:

- **Engage the audience.** Remember who you are speaking to (suspect, prospect, or customer/client), and make your content relevant and specific to them. If it's a live audience, get them to answer questions, raise their hands, stand up, or do something that engages them. In an ad, use personal, everyday conversation. Possibly the most powerful word you can use in advertising is "you." And if you can merge their actual name, it's even better! This is why you see marketers use your name in the subject line of an e-mail.

- **Get emotional.** Customers *always* buy on emotion. They justify with logic. Emotion motivates, not information. Their response is based on how they *feel*. Charge the copy with emotion, not just dry information.

- **Benefits.** Be sure to communicate in terms of what your product or service *does* for them, not just what it is. What are the benefits to them?

- **Lots of content is okay.** You may have learned or assumed that it is not good to put too much information in an ad. In advertising, the more you tell, the more you sell (it's just the opposite in sales). Those who are interested in what you are offering want more information. And you don't want to leave something out that may motivate them to act. Remember, we aren't talking about face-to-face here. When face-to-face, you want to limit the amount of information you give and ask questions.

- **Build the experience.** Much of the copywriting you may do will be for newsletters, articles, and things of that nature. You have the opportunity to build on your UEP™ (Unique Experience Proposition™).

- **Use testimonials and endorsements.** Real words from real clients and endorsements from highly influential people is some of the best copy you can use. I work with the Ziglar, Inc. which is the most trusted name in the training industry. I have a video of myself with Dr. John C. Maxwell, the world's number one leadership expert. In the video, he validates me as a leader. These are both examples that build credibility.

- **Use the Thirteen Most Powerful Words in Advertising.** The following words are said to be the most effective words in advertising. It's easy to see why.

1. **Discover** (This word is experiential in nature.)

2. **Easy** (Everyone wants easy today.)

3. **Guarantee** (No one wants to be stuck with something they're unhappy with.)

4. **Health** (Everyone wants to be healthy.)

5. **Love** (There's an emotional word for you.)

6. **Money** (This is important to everyone.)

7. **New** (You see this one used by Madison Avenue constantly!)

8. **Proven** (This word demonstrates they aren't going to be the guinea pig!)

9. **Results** (This creates social proof, which is very important.)

10. **Safety** (What's the opposite of safe? Danger!)

11. **Save** (Everyone is interested in saving time, money, or energy.)

12. **You** (This is the most powerful word in advertising, according to my good friend and marketing consultant David Frey.)

13. **FREE** (People say there's no free lunch, but watch them line up for free stuff!)

- **Create a sense of urgency.** To motivate your audience to action, you must create a sense of urgency. This may be through using an expiration date for an offer, a limited supply, or simply the loss factor that occurs by not taking action.

  - For example, if you want to start saving money now, "get this product before the offer expires on..." In this simple example, the benefit is saving money (and depending on how much space you have in your advertising piece, you want to go deeper with the benefits of saving money). The sense of urgency comes in when you realize you are paying too much now. When? Now. And of course you must act before the expiration date. There are many ways to create a sense of urgency. I recommend that you understand how to do that in your message.

### 3. A Phenomenal Call to Action

Many sales messages and presentations fall short because there is no call to action. What do you want them to do? Call a phone number? Fill out a form? Make a specific change in their lives? Make sure you tell them exactly what to do and how to do it. Example: Go to this website right now and get your FREE CD!

## CHAPTER 14

# PHENOMENAL INTERNET MARKETING

Many small business owners aren't up to speed on what's happening online. At the same time, some of the younger business owners seem to think that everything should be digital. They dismiss anything offline as "old school," slow, and ineffective. The truth is in the middle (as usual). How *you* use the Internet to market your business really depends on your business and your target market, but here are seven minimum steps to follow.

## 1. Have at Least One Website

Your main site is your "branding" site. In other words, this tells your story. Remember, a brand is nothing more than what people say when you are not around. Guess who manages that? You do! Your brand has to come through loud and clear on your site. The first thing people do today when they learn about you is go to your site.

Will they fall in love? Will they run? There is no telling how much damage is being done to small businesses because of horrible websites. If a customer comes to your site and finds something old and tired, guess how they think about your business? You may not need the flashiest site around, but your image *does* need to be positive. Since you want to have fresh content, you may consider having a platform where you or someone else can post regular updates or have a social media plug-in.

## 2. Have an Opt-In

A huge mistake I see many small business owners make is not having an opt-in on their website. An opt-in is a way for prospects to give you their e-mail addresses so you can communicate with them. Offer something free that will benefit them (see "The Fastest Growth Tool on the Planet!" for examples). Don't ask for more than the first name and e-mail address at first, because many who visit your site may not be ready to give you a lot of information yet. So, just a contact page isn't good enough. You are asking for too much information without giving anything in return.

Have a compelling opt-in that offers a solution to your target market's biggest problem. "Sign Up for Our Free Newsletter" isn't compelling enough unless you tell them what the benefit of getting the newsletter is. On my main site, I offer free business-building tips by e-mail, free videos, and webinars. I ask only for the first name and e-mail address. But once the person clicks *submit*, he or she is taken to a page that offers something more valuable. At the time of this writing I am offering a free CD that is mailed. The audio program reveals the "Five Secrets of a Phe-nomenal Business." If your business isn't very phenomenal and you want it to be, then you'll order that! And we mail free CDs constantly. There are many things you can offer, but the key is to get something prominently posted on your site.

To take that up a notch, have an autoresponder (an automatic system that automatically sends an e-mail response to each person who opts-in immediately). You can customize this to say whatever you want it to say. And if you want to take it into the stratosphere, you can create a series of responses over time that brings them step by step to the sale, or takes them through a learning path.

By the way, this can be done for every product or service that you provide at every level. It can be as sophisticated as you want. I won't recommend specific programs here because, by the time you read this, they could be outdated. But there is no shortage of programs to choose from. This brings me to the next part of your Phenomenal Internet Marketing System...

## 3. Have a Regular Outgoing E-Mail Newsletter

An e-mail newsletter that adds value to your prospects and clients is a powerful tool. As you give them solutions to their problems and offer solutions that your competitors aren't even talking about, you position yourself as the "go-to" person in your industry.

## 4. Have a Strong Social Media Presence

At this point, in most cases, it's not whether you should use social media or not, it's which one(s) to use, and how to use them effectively. The way I see social media is like a worldwide networking group that's happening 24/7. Remember that all of business is about relationships. Using social media can help you build and deepen relationships.

Ironically, when I wrote this section to appear in *The 5 Secrets of a Phenomenal Business*, I was on the Sunshine Coast of Australia, overlooking the ocean from my balcony and I had my Facebook page open. I was communicating with people all around the world, and a business associate noticed I was in Australia and contacted me for lunch. Three hours later we were having lunch and set up a business deal. Networking and engaging people on social media doesn't mean you are just going after business deals. You are building relationships that may *become* business deals.

Use the social media platforms that your clients and referral sources are using. Instead of picking the one you like, find out where they are and plug in. Social media doesn't need to own your life either. Once you get familiar with posting, simply make a post once or twice a day (depending on your business and the platform). Always respond to comments, acknowledge retweets, etc. The key is engagement. Don't over promote. Remember, it's about building relationships. If you aren't going to do it, hire someone who will. I hired a marketing manager who does a phenomenal job keeping my social media up to date. She also handles just about every facet of marketing for my training company. Victoria is a Godsend. The more active your business is, the more time is required for marketing and you can't do it all yourself.

Your brand has to come through loud and clear on your site. The first thing people do today when they learn about you is go to your site. Will they fall in love? Will they run? If a customer comes to your site and finds something old and tired, guess how they think about your business?

## 5. Understand SEO

Search Engine Optimization (SEO) is optimizing your website so that search engines rank it as a superior site for keywords and terms. Most small businesses want to be number one on Google and most marketers and business consultants will tell you that's where you want to be. I'm going to be a little controversial here and say it may not be the most important thing in the world, and that ranking is *not* required to be successful in business.

If you are putting all your effort into SEO and not marketing to your past clients and calling on referral sources, I would say you have your priorities mixed up—depending on the business. If you have an online business, that's different.

Think and strategize before putting time and energy into SEO that you could be putting into building powerful referral sources. And by all means, *do not respond to the spammers* and telemarketers trying to sell you SEO services. Get a referral. And don't do it yourself if it is going to take you away from more important things.

## 6. Understand Paid Online Advertising

When it comes to Google Adwords, banner ads, and such, follow the guidelines in Phenomenal Direct Advertising and make sure you understand what your plan is! Do *not* get into the world of paid advertising without studying and understanding it. That's like showing up to a gunfight with a dull pocketknife!

## 7. Use a Branded E-Mail Address

When you are communicating with people, use an e-mail address that has your branding domain in it. Example: howard@

howardpartridge.com. Don't use a Gmail, MSN, or Yahoo e-mail to communicate with business associates, prospects or clients because it devalues your brand.

Having your website address present encourages people to visit your site. Also, have at least your contact info in your e-mail signature (address, phone, website, etc.), and maybe even an opt-in and a photo.

## CHAPTER 15

# PHENOMENAL DIRECT SALES

Finally, there's the age-old idea of actually making a sales call! Part marketing and part sales, direct selling is when you market directly to a prospect in person. Don't discount this process!

The fact that you are taking the time to speak to *one* person is not the issue, it's what can happen as a result. In the case of network marketing (also called multi-level marketing) for example, one person could build a huge team for you in the future. Perhaps it's a person who can become a monthly recurring client for you. My wife is in radio advertising sales. Outside of calling on ad agencies that she is assigned to, she has to actually *call* on someone! Imagine that!

If landing a client is worth the time investment of calling on someone in person, by all means do it. But do it well. And please consider the options I have shared with you so far before investing too much time in this process unless you have already developed a phenomenal system for it. In other words, you could invest the same amount of time with a referral source who can send you as many end-user clients as you want as it takes to land one end-user client. Also, make sure you have done your Client-Based Marketing before investing too much time developing this process.

Many companies have direct salespeople and do very well with this. Others, not so good. I get sick thinking about all the time that is wasted by inept salespeople. People walk into our office every day selling insurance or business products of some kind. The entertainment begins as we watch them drive up. The other day, the first thing one of them did was open his car door and spit a big hocker right on the parking lot! What a great first impression! He walked in the door and asks, "Is the owner in?" How lame!

This pitiful scenario repeats itself over and over every day. These poor guys obviously haven't been trained well (or at all). Most of them end up quitting, I'm sure. If they are successful, it's completely by accident. I don't know about you, but I don't want my success to be by accident! Many small businesses don't realize that they are failing because of a flawed system. Any strategy that has a chance of working has to be implemented properly. If an account is worth calling on, they are worth investing in.

So, here's what you do...walk in with the Secret Weapon (chocolates, doughnuts, candy, or whatever). If you are calling on a lot of people who may or may not be prospects and you can't afford to invest five bucks a call, then use this inexpensive technique: get some clear cellophane baggies with a ribbon from a package supplier. Put four or five pieces of regular candy inside and attach a business card.

Any strategy that has a chance of working has to be implemented properly. If an account is worth calling on, they are worth investing in.

Walk in and give it to the rejectionist (I mean receptionist!) and say, "Hi, I'm [your name], and I brought you some chocolates." She blushes, and you say, "What is your name?" She responds as she tries to gain her composure. "Well, Betty, our company is the most respected, experienced [whatever you do] in the area, and I just wanted to drop by and give you all a free gift [your Free Trial Offer]. Who would I need to talk to about that?"

How hard is that? The candy generates the permission you need to intrigue them with your free trial offer. That gives you the permission to share your UEP™, and if they take the Free Trial Offer, you get a presentation! If your presentation is any good and they are truly prospects, not suspects, you are now simply measuring time invested with closing rates. To be effective in direct selling, you first have to give them a compelling reason to meet with you.

Focus on becoming an asset to them and building a relationship. When you get an appointment, offer them your sales presentation (covered in *The 5 Secrets of a Phenomenal Business*). If you don't, get the decision maker's card and put that person on a follow-up system in Send Out Cards and develop a follow-up system.

## CHAPTER 16

# THE SEVEN M'S OF PHENOMENAL MARKETING

Now that you have an idea of the kinds of systems and strategies that are required for a relationship-based marketing system that can create record sales and profits for your business, you need a focused plan.

An easy way to think about your marketing planning is to use the Seven M's of Phenomenal Marketing. The Seven M's are:

## The First M: Your Phenomenal Marketing Mindset

Most small business owners focus on the technical work of their business, or giving good customer service, and market only when they are forced to. As I write this, I'm in Italy with a group of artists. The idea of having to market themselves drives them crazy! At the same time, they aren't happy being "starving artists." I think I'm finally getting through to them that if they are willing to learn the art of marketing, they can reach more of their dreams and goals in life, which for some of them is to just do more art.

Your Phenomenal Marketing Mindset is about understanding what marketing is. To recap what you learned earlier in this book: marketing is everything you do to attract prospects to your business. The function of marketing is to increase sales, and there are only three ways to increase sales: get a higher price, get more clients, and get more business from existing clients.

Remember that the ONLY reason your business exists is to be a vehicle to help you reach your life goals. That vehicle needs gasoline, which is sales. Nothing happens in a business unless a sale is made. A sale happens only when marketing is done, and profitable sales cure all other business evils. Your life goals will not be reached unless you make a profit. A business without a profit is just a hobby.

## The Second M: Your Phenomenal Money

The second M is your *money* goal. You want to set a sales goal for the next twelve months. If you have history, go back to see how much you did last year. Are you on a growth path? Are sales declining? What significant changes are taking place that can change those numbers? Once you have your annual sales goal, break it down by the month, by the week, and by the day (or as often as you have transactions). If you do large projects, break it down by the project. For example, some of my coaching clients have construction or remodeling businesses.

My brother owns a McDonald's, and his profit is determined by how the staff cost is managed by the hour. If you do a few large projects per year, then determine how many projects you are going to do and what the average project amount will be. If you sell products, how many products will be sold at what average price point?

You will also want to break down your sales goal by profit center (or service category) and even by how much you will do in repeat business, referral business, and direct sales and advertising. You will learn about this in *The 5 Secrets of a Phenomenal Business.*

To get to your sales goal, you will need to know what your *profit* goal is. It all starts with your net profit because that is what funds your life goal. Remember, the one and *only* reason your business exists is to be a vehicle to help you achieve your life goals.

A business without a profit is just a hobby! I don't know about you, but being broke and in debt isn't any fun. To top it off, working 24/7 to be broke and in debt is even worse! If you're going to be broke, you may as well stay home. At least you could enjoy yourself while you are going broke!

The wonderful thing about being a business owner is that you can plan what you want your profit to be. Lord willing, of course. None of us know what challenges life will bring us, but we would also be fools to build anything without a plan. So we plan and we work the plan the best that we possibly can. The amazing thing is that when you plan and stay focused, it works! Determine what you want your profit to be. Then you will have to determine your cost of doing business.

Also determine how much you are willing to *invest* in marketing. This should be in your Twelve-Month Cash Flow Budget.

Decide in *advance* what you are going to invest. This will keep you from becoming a victim of the advertising wolves in sheep's clothing. They have an irresistible offer that you are absolutely convinced will work (although it hasn't been proven).

It will also keep you from marketing only when you get slow. If you wait to market until you actually "need" the income, it's too late. Work your marketing system continuously.

A marketing investment amount that includes exactly how much you will invest in each system, strategy, and ad will keep you focused rather than reacting to circumstances. Far too often, marketing is done in purely an opportunistic manner rather than a focused plan.

Another thing I have learned from the countless surveys we have taken from the small business owners we coach is that there isn't nearly enough invested in marketing. When you see the puny line item called marketing on an income statement, it's no wonder there isn't any business!

You have to plant a seed to get a crop! As the late Jim Rohn (who was considered one of America's foremost business philosophers) said, "You can't say to a field, 'give me a crop and then I'll plant a seed.' You can't say to a fireplace, 'give me heat and then I'll give you some wood!'" It's ridiculous, yet that's what I see every day.

Decide in advance what you are going to invest in marketing. Commit to that investment. Don't make the investment based on whether you have "extra" money or not. Put it in the budget. Make the investment. I know that planning and budgeting doesn't sound like much fun, but it can make you wildly wealthy, which means you can go have all kinds of fun!

**You have to plant a seed to get a crop!**

How much do you invest in marketing? Whatever it's going to take to get the profit number you need. You may need to do some research on this, but once you line out the things you are going to implement, figure out how much those items will cost. To get this exactly right, you will have to go adjust your 12-Month Cash Flow Budget.

## The Third M: Your Phenomenal Mission

In Chapter 2 of *The 5 Secrets of a Phenomenal Business*, I shared the importance of having a *mission*. When it comes to marketing, you want to keep in mind what you are actually delivering. If you have not determined what your mission is, you should come to terms with that before planning your marketing. Your mission will determine who your target market is and what your marketing messages will look like.

And keep in mind that if you aren't passionate about the mission you are on, you won't promote it well and you won't lead others to carry it out either.

Your mission is the unique experience you want to deliver. For example, at Phenomenal Products, our mission is to help small business owners stop being slaves to their businesses. Although this is a marketing book, and two of my other books are mostly personal development books, our specific mission is to help small business owners who are stuck.

Are you passionate about the difference you can make? When small business owners stop being slaves to their businesses and have more freedom to spend time with their families, and do the things they love, it really turns me on. That's why I get up in the morning. It's why I'm writing this book now. It's why I'm willing to travel around the world and sacrifice sleep, and do things that are difficult and inconvenient. I could just stay at the beach in Destin or enjoy time at my dream home in Houston, but I don't. This is what I'm called to. What is your calling?

## The Fourth M: Your Phenomenal Market

To determine who your prime target market is, think about who wants and needs the unique experience you want to provide. For example, back to Phenomenal Products' mission to help small business owners stop being slaves to their businesses. Our target market is the small business owner who is open to change and ready to learn. This is only *one* type of business owner. Not every business owner is our market.

For example, the "serial entrepreneur" is not our prime target. The serial entrepreneur is the one who is always starting a new venture, has a very short attention span, and gets distracted by "bright shiny objects." They are just looking for the next big marketing wave to ride. That's not what I do. Although the solid marketing strategies I am sharing in this book have been validated by some of the world's top business trainers, and have worked for my companies and small businesses around the world, serial entrepreneurs won't slow down long enough to make them work. Does that mean we don't service serial entrepreneurs? Not at all; we just don't target them.

Another type of business owner is the brand-new business owner. The problem here is that they have not yet experienced the pain of being in business. They don't feel like a slave. They are still on the "honeymoon," so to speak.

When I learned who my target market was, I was more successful, because I then focused all my marketing and my coaching around the needs of my prime target market.

Another example is my high-end service company in Houston. We decided that we would provide the "most outstanding service experience ever"—that we would have the best equipment and processes, we would be more trained than anyone else. We would offer first-class, over-the-top customer service. Guess what? Not everyone is willing to pay for that experience. So, our target market became what we call "Mercedes Clients." It doesn't mean they all drive Mercedes', it just means that they have a Mercedes *attitude* toward their indoor environment.

Another way to determine your prime target market comes from my friend Ellen Rohr, a phenomenal small business consultant. She says, "Picture your favorite customer—you know, the one who pays your price (and pays on time!). The one you love working with." Those are your perfect niche clients. Do you have a picture in mind? What are their frustrations? What is the competition doing to frustrate them?

What is their lifestyle? With whom do they associate? Where do they live? How much money do they make? How old are they? Are they business owners? How long have they been in business? Multiple locations or single location? Retail or wholesale?

Do you see how we could fill an entire book just with questions on how to know your niche market? One of the most important questions is how they buy. This will be vital when you get into "Methods" in a moment.

## The Fifth M: Your Phenomenal Message

Once you determine how much *money* your business needs to produce, what your *mission* is, and who your target *market* is, you now want to craft a *message* that resonates with them. Go back to the "Five-Point UEP" (Unique Experience Proposition™). This will become the core of your message. You should be able to expand and contract this message based on the situation and the *method* of marketing you are using.

If you are at a networking group that gives you sixty seconds of speaking time, you can use the full Five-Point UEP. If you are writing an ad, or you are doing a sales presentation, you'll need to expand the five points. It is also vital to understand how to write marketing copy.

What's the message that resonates with your target market? The five-point "experiential" marketing message I shared with you earlier will fit any company wanting to provide a high-end service experience, but you want to pinpoint the exact emotional state they are in. You want to "join the conversation" happening in their head.

One of the things I found that really resonates with my target audience is "the number one reason small businesses don't grow or do as well as they could is F.T.I. (Failure to Implement)." For some crazy reason, this little axiom sticks in their mind and resonates at the highest level. My service company starts off with "avoid uneducated, uninformed and sometimes downright unscrupulous service companies…"

Who is going to respond to that? People who have tried the rest and now want to use the best!

> The number one reason small businesses don't grow or do as well as they could is F.T.I. (Failure to Implement).

## The Sixth M: Your Phenomenal Methods

What methods of marketing will you use to reach your phenomenal target market? You can have plenty of money to invest, a powerful, passionate, meaningful mission, a clearly defined target market, and a compelling message that sells like crazy, but if your perfect prospect never sees it, what's it worth?

What methods will best deliver the message they need? In order to determine this, we must ask ourselves a few questions. How does your prime target market buy services? Online? Offline? Through ads, direct mail, radio, television, newspaper? Do they read trade magazines? Are there online forums where they hang out? Do they primarily buy through referrals? If so, who do they trust? Who has a relationship with them?

I have seen too many small business owners who have a great product or service, but they struggle because they are using the wrong media. Understanding how your perfect target market buys is vital to choosing the right method to reach them.

I hope this book has given you lots of ideas on what methods to use. In most small businesses, the simplest, most effective way is to use my Referral Marketing system of identifying potential referral sources, bring your phenomenal message about your

What methods of marketing will you use to reach your phenomenal target market? You can have plenty of money to invest, a powerful, passionate, meaningful mission, a clearly defined target market, and a compelling message that sells like crazy, but if your perfect prospect never sees it, what's it worth?

phenomenal mission to them, and inspire them to talk about you to their clients (your perfect target market).

Once they refer, you then have a phenomenal Client-Based Marketing system using something like Send Out Cards, which compels them to come back to you and to refer you. I have found that companies that learn how to use Referral Marketing and Client-Based Marketing well can be very successful without direct advertising or direct sales.

I had dinner with an SEO guy not too long ago and he was telling me about the client he helped get to number one on Google. But the client is still struggling financially. He doesn't have enough business. I could clearly see that in his industry, all he has to do is begin developing a relationship with powerful referral sources. He also is not marketing to his past clients. Big mistake.

I cannot stress enough the importance of a phenomenal Referral Marketing system and a phenomenal Client-Based Marketing system! Couple that with a phenomenal mission and message— and you have a winning combination!

## The Seventh M: Your Phenomenal M.A.P. (Marketing Action Plan)

Finally, to get where you want to go, you need a map. Your Marketing Action Plan outlines what you are going to do every day, every week, and every month to reach your goals.

You could also call this your Marketing Calendar. It doesn't have to be fancy, it just has to be. You need a road map to follow. When you take the time to create a simple plan, you can then easily follow it.

When you've done the first six M's, this part becomes much easier.

Every M.A.P. will be different, but here's an example:

*Daily*

- Send Thank You Letters or Cards

- Post on Social Media Three Times Per Day

- Send One Heartfelt Greeting Card

- Send All Birthday and Anniversary Cards

- Reminder Letters

- Reminder Calls

- On-Site Consultation Confirmation Letters

- Confirmation Calls

- Confirmation E-Mails

- Quality Check Calls

- Quality Check E-Mails

- Referral Certificates

*Weekly*

- Send E-Mail Newsletter

- Post on Blog

- Update Online Listings and Banner Ads

- Attend Networking Groups
- One-on-One Meetings

*Monthly*

- Client Newsletter or Send Out Cards
- Referral Source Newsletter or Send Out Cards
- Referral Source Visits

## CHAPTER 17

# THE 14 FASTEST WAYS TO THE CASH IN ANY BUSINESS!

Okay, this is what you've been waiting for: the fourteen things you can do right now to generate cash. This list does not include paid advertising. The reason? Because paid advertising takes money, time, and testing. I don't want you to spend a lot of money trying to figure out what works and what doesn't. If you have paid advertising you've done in the past that has worked extremely well, and you aren't currently doing it, I would encourage you to consider that. If you do, be sure to implement it exactly how you did it when it was successful. You see, the idea here is to duplicate what works.

We know the following fourteen things work. Implement each and EVERY one of these as FAST as you can. They are in order according to ease of implementation, but do all of them as quickly as you can for best results.

## FASTEST WAY TO THE CASH #1:
## Set and Post Your Sales Goal

We talked about this earlier in the book. Do it now (even if you haven't done your twelve-month budget). You probably have a good idea of how much needs to be coming in. Set it there for now. You can adjust it later. You may think this isn't an important strategy to put cash in your pocket fast, but as a person who has reached many, many goals and dreams, I can tell you it works.

Why does it work? Because when you put something into your conscious mind, your subconscious mind begins to work on making it a reality. Post your goal where you can see it *every* day, *several* times per day. You may want to post it in several places. When you begin to study goal setting and visualizing your goals, you'll find that this is a phenomenon that, when ignored, costs you real money. Not to mention many goals and dreams. Do it. Do it now.

Then begin tracking your success. Each day, post on a whiteboard or in a notebook how much you did in sales. Post it where you can see it every day, several times per day. This is a proven process. Go ahead and put down what you did yesterday in sales. If you have staff members, record their sales as well and post them. Do it now.

## FASTEST WAY TO THE CASH #2:
## Answer Your Phone LIVE

Any phone call that you capture that was a potentially lost sale will increase your sales. The following is an excerpt from my book *The 5 Secrets of a Phenomenal Business* that discusses the importance of the subject:

### Avoiding the Silent Kiss of Death

Every day small businesses are suffering from what I call the "silent kiss of death." The silent kiss of death is when a prospect tries to do business with a company and the owner doesn't even know it! If someone calls your company during business hours and gets voice mail rather than speaking to a person, you're taking a chance of losing that prospect. Many prospects (like me) will hang up and forget about it or call someone else. It doesn't matter if you have Caller ID. By the time you call me back I'm probably off to other things.

If I walk into your store or restaurant and no one is there to greet me, guess what? Some customer types are going to turn around and walk right out. The sad thing is that many times these are the types of clients you want. People who are decisive.

I was reading one of John Maxwell's books, and he shared a story about a time when he and Margaret were in the drive-thru at Krispy Kreme. They love Krispy Kreme when they're hot, but when they drove by the "hot light" wasn't on. They decided to drive through anyway; and to their surprise, the doughnuts were piping hot. When he asked the person at the window why the light wasn't on, she replied, "We get too busy when the light is on, so I didn't turn it on."

If you're like me, I can't imagine how people could think that way, but they do. And it is up to us to train our people. We must train them why it is important to capture as many customers as we can when things are hot. This gets us through the lean times.

*Profitable sales cure all other business evils.* We need to close as many sales as possible because we are not only squandering the time, energy, and money that was invested in marketing, but we also want to make sure we have reserves for the "evils" that come our way—when we have to pay more tax than planned, something gets damaged, an employee costs us money, someone doesn't pay his bill, the economy tanks, or any other number of things that are completely out of our control. As my friend and author of *The Facts of Business Life* Bill McBean says, "Planning is not predicting the future, it's preparing for it."

### Have a Phenomenal Greeting

When people walk into your practice, your store, your restaurant, or call your company, you want to have an enthusiastic greeting that demonstrates you are excited to hear from them. And you should be!

So have a phenomenal greeting when people enter your facility or call your company.

I learned from Zig Ziglar many years ago to answer the telephone with "It's a great day at..." Of course, you might want to update that to "It's a phenomenal day at..." (smile). Remember that your callers make several important assumptions about your company when they call.

They are listening to confirm that you will live up to the marketing message. They are making judgments about the value of your service, whether you know what you are doing, and whether you can be trusted or not. When the telephone is not handled properly, you can needlessly create a negative impression that now has to be overcome.

More telephone answering tips:

- Speak slowly and clearly. Your caller may not be listening closely.

- Never answer with "hello" (even your cell phone). A friend may have given a prospect your cell phone number (and why do we answer so negative when it is a family member?).

- Never allow a child or a family member answer your business phone unless they are properly trained.

- Never, *ever* answer with "Can you hold please?" This tells callers they are not important.

- Be upbeat and positive *always!*

- You may want to use a mirror. A smile comes through the phone.

- Eliminate background noise, music, dogs, kids. This can be distracting and takes away from the experience for the client.

- Ask the caller his or her name, write it down, and use the name from that point on.

## FASTEST WAY TO THE CASH #3:
### Up-sell Every Order

Here's another excerpt from *The 5 Secrets of a Phenomenal Business:*

### How to Double Your Profit with the Most Profitable Sale Ever!

In any business there is one type of sale that brings the most profit. There is one single sales activity that can make the most difference in the profitability of your company. *Not taking advantage of this all-important sales opportunity will cost you thousands of dollars.*

The most profitable sale ever made is called the "up-sell" or "add-on" sale. Why is it the most profitable sale ever? Because you have already invested the time, money, and energy acquiring and serving your client. Therefore, anything that is added to the "ticket" is extremely profitable. This makes the up-sell the most profitable sale you can make.

### Why Most Small Business Owners Don't Up-sell

Have you been guilty of not making the up-sell in the past? I have. Why is that? Here are the reasons I have found that up-sells aren't made (by the owner *and* staff):

#### Pushy salesperson

You don't want to appear as the "used car salesman" stereotype. I will share with you in just a moment that you are actually doing your customer wrong by not offering the up-sell. I will prove it to you and you will agree, so stay with me.

Our view of a salesperson has likely been skewed as we grew up. We have been conditioned to believe that all salespeople are con artists. Maybe we grew up seeing salespeople take the discretionary income from our families. You must see yourself as a consultant who is looking out for your clients.

#### Fear

Somewhere along the way we have picked up the fear of rejection and we don't really know where it comes from. When we get confidence through sales training, we have goals, we have a system that we follow, and we have the desire to reach our goals and take the best care of our clients, we can have the focus to move forward even in the midst of fear.

Do you remember the acronym for FEAR? False Evidence Appearing Real. Your wonderful imagination is creating emotional images. They are almost always false, but appear real because of the way our minds work. Winners don't lack fear, they proceed in the face of it.

### Lack of training

Sales training gives you confidence. If you have staff, they must be trained in sales and presenting the products and services properly.

### No system

You should have scripts and procedures that are followed consistently. When you develop the right system that consistently works, it is then up to you to consistently implement it.

### Lack of goals

If you do not have clearly defined, compelling financial goals, you are less likely to do all you can in this area. It's a human fact. If your life goals don't require money, hopefully the cost to your client will motivate you to make the sale. You may have employees who have not connected their financial position to their future and may have "stinkin' thinkin'" about money. If so, that will limit the possibilities. You need to help them expand their money mindset.

### Busy

We are all busy today, but let me ask you a question, "If you don't make the most profitable sale ever and spend your time on less profitable activities, isn't it costing you *more* time to *not* up-sell?" Ponder that for a moment.

**Not making the up-sell is doing your customer WRONG!**

How is it possible that not up-selling is doing your customer an injustice? Let me ask you another question, "If your client doesn't use your extra services, will it *cost* them anything?" If not, you shouldn't be selling it. There is obviously a gain from purchasing your product or service, so there must be a cost if they don't.

Also, if they don't buy it from you and they learn about it from your competitor, how do you feel about that? Are all of your competitors honest and ethical? How do you feel about them taking care of your customer rather than you?

Finally, do you have a phenomenal reputation? Do you have experience? Are you educated in your field and do you educate your clients? Do you provide a phenomenal customer service experience? Do you stand behind your product?

Then wouldn't you agree that if they don't get to take advantage of all you have to offer, you are actually doing them wrong by not at least letting them know about it? It is their decision, but you are the consultant. As advisors, it is our job to share the opportunity with them.

## How Much Money Are You Leaving on the Table?

Think about how much you could potentially add to your business each day in add-on sales if you or your people were trained and focused. Now multiply that by five days a week. Now multiply that by fifty-two weeks per year. Now multiply that by the number of sales or service representatives you have. A mere $100 per day x 5 days per week is $26,000 per year. If I have ten representatives, that's $260,000 per year!

And speaking of staff, I recommend giving them an incentive on the add-on sale. I know there may be some "purists" who disagree, and that's okay if you do. But wouldn't it be nice to give them a "raise" without having to pay more and more just for them to exist? Sooner or later, the business isn't sustainable because we continue to give raises without increasing profits.

## How to Make Up-sells Consistently

First, you must train yourself in sales. This is a worthy endeavor. Get everything you can from the Zig Ziglar Corporation on sales training. Train your staff. Zig always said, "Everyone in the company may not be in sales, but anyone can cost the company a sale!"

And by the way, what if the receptionist asked a question like, "Did you get the XYZ product? It's really amazing!" The receptionist can then help make a sale. That brings me to the next point.

### Ask Questions

Remember that selling isn't telling. And telling isn't selling. Determine the additional items you have to offer. In the interview process, include some questions that will reveal the prospect's beliefs about that product or service. Ask questions that bring up that conversation.

Here's an example: The first business I started is a high-end cleaning firm that cares for stone floors, Oriental rugs, and fine textiles. The most profitable and most valuable up-sell is sealer for the stone and fabric protector for the textiles. We built questions into the script such as, "Did you get protector the last time you had this cleaned?" We don't sell it at that moment, instead we gather information (the more they tell, the more you sell).

Later on, during Step Five, we outline that the solution includes sealer or fabric protector. Not having investment furnishings protected costs the client big time down the road, yet many companies fail to even mention it. The result is the customer's property is at risk and the company doesn't make the profit it could. The owner doesn't reach his or her life goals, which may include passing on some of those profits to a good cause. Can you see how this all fits together in a phenomenal business?

Once you have opened the conversation, ask for permission to share more. Once you get that permission, you can go into a full interview on that particular service or product. If demonstrations or a free trial is appropriate, be sure to offer that.

A final note...don't offer *anything* until you have established rapport with the client and you have secured *believability*. You must establish yourself as a trusted consultant and representative before attempting an extra sale. Many times this is accomplished by WOWing the client with the primary service or product first.

## FASTEST WAY TO THE CASH #4:
### Call Twenty Past Clients Per Day

You learned earlier in this book that not marketing to your past clients is "the biggest marketing mistake of all." The good

When people walk into your practice, your store, your restaurant, or call your company, you want to have an enthusiastic greeting that demonstrates you are excited to hear from them. And you should be! So have a phenomenal greeting when people enter your facility or call your company.

news is that you don't have to spend a ton of money to market to them. In fact, a good old-fashioned phone call will do.

Over the years, my coaching clients have found that doing this simple thing has helped them increase their sales significantly. Start with the people who are overdue for service or that you haven't seen in a while. If you don't have your customer base on a database, then find their invoices, or anything that has their phone number on it. If you did not record their address and e-mail, this will be a good time to get it.

What do you say when you call them? There are many scripts. Use the one that is most appropriate for your business and culture. In Texas, I would simply call someone up and tell them I was thinking about them and thought I would call and see how they are doing. In the southern states, that would work just fine. But recently I was teaching in the UK, and the audience members, who were mostly male (with female clients), thought it might be awkward. No problem. There are several scripts you can use:

- "We are calling to update our records…" This is a great way to get information (such as an e-mail address) that you did not gather previously.

- "We are calling to let you know about our new referral reward program…"

- "We are calling to let you know about our special offer…"

- "We are calling to let you know that it has been over [enter the timeframe your client should frequent your business] since we've seen you…"

## FASTEST WAY TO THE CASH #5:
## Close More Sales by Overcoming Price Objections

I teach a 7 step sales process in my training program that builds rapport, connects with the prospect's emotional state, establishes credibility, and then dives into problems and solutions. Once all of that is done, the investment is quoted. All along the way, I teach that asking questions is the key.

If you could close more prospects by getting really good at overcoming price objections, you would put more cash in your bank account. Not closing the sale causes you to work HARDER. Here's an excerpt from my book *The 5 Secrets of a Phenomenal Business* about overcoming price objections:

> In the best of situations, you will have already overcome all objections during Step Five. If not, this is where you will need to apply this skill. Did you notice the word I just used? Skill. To be a phenomenal business owner and sales consultant, you need skill that requires training. Train yourself with information, seminars, and coaching.

**When you get an objection, ALWAYS ask a question. ALWAYS!**

If there was ever a time when questions were important in the sales process, it is in this step. When you get an objection, always ask a question. Always. What kind of question? Well, what if you simply repeated the objection in the form of a question?

For example, if the prospect says, "Wow, that's expensive!" you say, "So you feel it's expensive?" They now have to respond. Remember, the more *they* tell, the more *you* sell. They might just say, "Yes, it's expensive." To which you respond with, "Would you mind sharing what you mean by too expensive?" Your goal is to get more information about their objection.

There are literally hundreds of closing techniques and questions you could use, so I recommend you study Zig Ziglar's *Secrets of Closing the Sale* CDs as well as anything else he produced on the subject. Again, you want to develop your skill in this area.

## Five Ways to Overcome Price Objections

If you have come all the way to this step, the only objection you should have is "price." Here are my five favorite ways to overcome price objections:

### 1. Review the value.

The reason you went through the Seven Step Sales System is so you can go back to the agreement points in Step Five. If you assessed the market correctly and you know that you offer more value for the investment, go back and connect with that. Reconnect them with your five point message. Confirm that they truly want to work with a company that has the unique qualities your company has and that they truly want to get the benefits you offer.

Perhaps they are convinced they can get "the same thing" somewhere else. Obviously, you didn't convince them of the uniqueness of your product or service and the value, so you now must do that.

Get their permission to explore the other options with them. For example, let's say they are buying a service, and they have used your competitors in the past. Ask them why they didn't call that company to start with. Why have they called you? Perhaps you will find out that the other company can't service them when they need to, or they've gone out of business, they can't remember their phone number, or whatever.

You can now ask a question like, "Why do you think that is?" In other words, perhaps they can't service you or they went out of business because they didn't charge enough. The question is, "Do you want to have a company that you can rely on over and over again?"

If they are comparing you to another competitor that charges a lower price, you want to ask questions that will cause them to wonder what the other company is leaving out. What is their true reputation? What kind of experience do they really have? Are they really trained? Can they really and truly deliver the experience you want? And do they stand behind their work?

If you are telling me they can do all of this for a cheaper price and there is nothing different, you better get scheduled with them quickly before they go out of business! I mean, really, isn't that just the plain truth? You know it and I know it. You get what you pay for, and companies that charge too little cannot deliver consistently for very long.

You must create contrast between you and them, and create doubt without mentioning any competitor by name. And you must attract the kinds of prospects in your marketing that you have a chance to close. Don't try to sell a KIA customer a Mercedes, and don't try to sell a Mercedes client a KIA!

## 2. Offer payment options.

If you haven't determined what their budget is (if they have one), you want to do that now. Depending on your industry, you may want to put that in the interview process in Step Four. If not, when you get a price objection, ask, "What were you planning on investing in this project/product?" If they don't know, it means they don't have a basis for judging the pricing. They probably haven't been shopping.

At this point, you have a couple of options. If you can get them to give you a figure, try this option. Let's say the investment is $500 and they didn't want to spend more than $350. You say, "How would it be if you could put the three fifty down today and pay the rest later?" My experience has been that if they really want your product or service (and that is the key: building desire in the presentation), they will find a way to pay for it if they don't feel they can afford it today.

Of course, you want to mention that you accept major credit cards. Although I don't like to help people get into debt, and I'm a big fan of Dave Ramsey (Dave helps people get out of debt), I do allow people to use credit cards to pay for my products and services (Dave doesn't). If I was in Dave's business, I'm sure I would only allow debit cards like he does.

If they want your product, work with them on the payment options by first determining how much they can put down today. If you can cover your hard costs on the first installment, you haven't lost anything even if they never pay you. If they don't buy, you may have lost a client forever. So, my goal is to close today. If you are convinced your product or service will really help them, you should have a strong desire to close as well.

### 3. Referral Reward Program.

Another strategy is to show them how they can get their entire investment back by using your referral reward program. Simply ask, "Did you know you can get all of your money back with our referral reward program?" Share how the program works and how they get their money back. For example: "Mrs. Prospect, we offer a 10 percent referral reward for any new client you send us. That means that once you have sent just ten new clients, you will have gotten all of your money back on this project." I have found that some people who truly can't afford my product or service will work extra hard at getting referrals for me so they can get my service. Again, it's about creating desire for your product.

### 4. Down sell.

With this strategy, you will offer a lower priced product or change the scope of the project. You settle for less money today, but you did not lower your price! If you lower your price without attaching it to a condition, you lose all credibility! In their mind, you could have offered the lower price to start with. Keep in mind that people will ask for a lower price simply because they know many salespeople will immediately drop the price. Don't do it if you want to maintain trust.

Let's say you are selling fitness training. You have presented the value of a package that includes X number of weeks in group training and a few one-on-one sessions. You could take out some of the sessions. You are still selling training at a profitable rate, just settling for a lower package today.

**5. Offer a free trial.**

Earlier, I revealed the Free Trial Offer Program. Not only is it a phenomenal marketing tool, it can also be a phenomenal closing tool. Many times your prospects don't know how to value your product or service and they can't imagine how good it is. Therefore, allow them to experience it for free if you can. If you can't actually give them a sample, create some sort of experience that allows them to see and feel exactly what it will be like.

Also in the marketing chapter I talked about the "free ride" Lexus gives its prospects. Chick-fil-A was the first to offer free samples in the mall. Now everyone does it. If you have a cleaning company, for example, offer to clean an area free as a sample. If you have a high-value product or service, you may want to borrow a tactic from the time-share industry. Have you ever been on vacation and noticed a little booth or office that advertises a free resort stay or a free Jet-Ski rental? In order to get the freebie, you have to listen to a ninety-minute presentation. And guess what? It works! Of course, you'll leave out the high pressure that some of those outfits use.

## Creating a Sense of Urgency

Earlier, I briefly covered that you need to create a sense of urgency in your message. In marketing, you create a sense of urgency to respond. In sales, you also need to create a sense of urgency to close.

The reason is that the level of desire can wane after the presentation is over. The emotion dissipates. Remember that all sales are made on emotion. Some prospects will not close right away, and understanding the behavior styles and when to close or not will be part of your ongoing training. One technique you can use in those cases is to go ahead and do the paperwork, but put it on hold until a certain date.

It goes like this. "Mr. Prospect, I understand that you want to think about it. At the same time, I know you've expressed interest in the special offer, correct?" "What if we do this...let's go ahead and do the paperwork, and we'll put a hold on it for you so you will have time to think about it. If you decide not to move forward, we'll shred the paperwork. How does that sound?"

I have seen this work many times. Your testing will show how many end up cancelling and how many don't. By the way, you then work on a suitable date (not next month!) and you put a date on the paperwork and ask about processing the payment tomorrow (or whenever it is) if you don't hear from the prospect. You want to avoid having to track down the person. Put the follow-up responsibility on the prospect. Remember once more: if your product or service benefits the person, there is no harm in working hard to help close the sale!

## FASTEST WAY TO THE CASH #6:
### Send a Client Survey

One of the best ways to reach out to past clients is with what I call a Client Survey. This is a survey that you send and/or e-mail to your existing clients to find out how they feel about your business.

Send a survey to all clients, regardless of when they purchased from you. The idea is to engage them.

There are three major benefits of a Client Survey:

1.  **Generate testimonials.** The Client Survey Form has an area for testimonials, which provide powerful marketing copy for other uses.

2.  **Get service feedback.** An unsatisfied customer will tell more people about their experience than a satisfied customer will. But they won't tell you unless you ask. The Client Survey uncovers any service issues and helps you avoid negative reviews. Also, many times a client who had a negative experience that has been fixed becomes a more loyal client because there is no doubt that you care and will make it right.

3.  **Makes your business better.** By having the client rate individual parts of the service experience, you can improve the areas of your business that get less than a perfect rating.

How does sending a Client Survey make you fast cash? A Client Survey engages your client and proves that you care about them. The survey also talks about your referral program. Every touch you make with past clients increases your chances of repeat and referral business. Our experience has been that a blanket survey generates results.

You can also add a Special Offer with the Client Survey to create a sense of urgency. Example: "Return this survey by <insert date> and get <insert special offer>."

Dear Friend and Client,

Thank you for using our service or product. We want to know how we are doing in *your* eyes. Please let us know if you were thrilled, simply satisfied, or disappointed. This information will help us accomplish our mission: **To provide our clients with the most outstanding service experience ever!**™

Directions: After each question please write the number corresponding to the answer that best reflects your opinion. *Write N/A if not sure or not applicable.

| Very Dissatisfied | | | | Very Satisfied |
|---|---|---|---|---|
| 1 | 2 | 3 | 4 | 5 |

1.  How satisfied are you with the following aspects of your service or product experience?

    a.  On-time arrival _____

    b.  Courteous on the job site _____

    c.  Quality of service or product _____

    d.  Responsiveness to your special requests _____

    e.  Telephone courtesy _____

    f.  Responsiveness of staff _____

    g.  Schedule availability _____

    h.  Amount of information offered _____

    i.  Overall performance _____

    j.  Our reputation _____

      k.  Our experience \_\_\_\_

      l.  Our guarantee \_\_\_\_

2. What did you like MOST about [Your Company Name]?

3. What did you like LEAST about [Your Company Name]?

4. After using our service or product, are you more or less likely to use us again?

      a. Less likely \_\_\_\_

      b. More likely \_\_\_\_

5. After using [Your Company Name], are you more or less likely to refer someone to us?

      a.  Less likely \_\_\_\_

      b.  More likely \_\_\_\_

6. Are you aware of the [Your Company Name] Referral Reward Program?

      Yes \_\_\_\_ No \_\_\_\_

Additional Comments:

Name (optional) _____

Telephone number _____

May we use your testimonial for promotional purposes?

Yes _____ No _____

If yes, please sign here_____

**[Your Company]** will read all customer comments. Thank you for helping us accomplish our mission.

Three Easy Ways to Return This Form:

1. Fax: [Your Fax Number]

2. Mail: [Your Company Name and Address]

3. Web: Go to [Your Company Website Address] and click "Client Survey Form"

**THE [YOUR COMPANY NAME] GUARANTEE**

If you were not completely thrilled with the service or product experience you received from us, we will rush back to your location to remedy the situation. If you are still unimpressed, you owe us nothing and we will issue a 100% refund. Thank you!

## FASTEST WAY TO THE CASH #7:
## Implement Your Referral Reward Program

Let your clients know about your Referral Reward Program by phone, mail, and e-mail. Tell every client, guest, member, or patient about it when they buy from you.

## FASTEST WAY TO THE CASH #8:
## Implement Your Free Trial Offer Program

Now, every time you meet someone, someone visits your website, or you get a group of people together, you have a powerful way to not only build your list, but to communicate with a larger number of prospects. The more prospects you have and the more qualified they are, the more money you are likely to make.

## FASTEST WAY TO THE CASH #9:
## Market to Past Referral Sources

You have probably been referred by great referral sources in the past, but until you read this book, you may not have realized the potential in building that relationship deeper.

Make a list of every source who has referred you in the past. You may need to go back to your records. Put them on a list and call them up, and/or go by to see them. In-person visits are best. Also, mail them something of value as well.

Reconnecting with these referral sources can not only generate immediate cash, but you can now begin building a stronger, longer term relationship.

## FASTEST WAY TO THE CASH #10:
# Send a Thank You Letter Package to Every Client Immediately After the Purchase

Sending a thank you letter or Send Out Card along with the Client Survey and an outline of your Referral Reward Program will go a long way to build client loyalty, and you are likely to generate more referrals.

Most of all, this will help you uncover any service issues that may have been overlooked. Ninety percent of unsatisfied customers will never let you know, they will simply use someone else. Remember, increasing your customer retention rate and reducing your customer attrition rate makes you more money!

Here's how it helps you get cash faster: One of the strongest opportunities to generate referrals from a client is when they are still feeling the positive emotion of using your product or service. Also, they now trust you and have a stronger rapport with you, and will likely buy additional services or products.

The timing of just after the purchase is a short window that you must take advantage of.

## FASTEST WAY TO THE CASH #11:
## Implement Your Five-Point Marketing Message

How will this put "fast cash" in your pocket? When your message is compelling, exciting and interesting, it goes viral. Keep working on it until everyone in your industry is talking about you.

## FASTEST WAY TO THE CASH #12:
### Dress for Success

Here's another one you might discount at first blush, but let me ask you a question: "If you tell me about your service and I'm in the market, but I don't trust you because of the way you are dressed, doesn't that cost you money?"

If your attitude is that people should "accept" you the way you are, you're in for a shocker. That might be okay in life—we all select the "community" we want to be a part of—but it's a death trap in business.

You are coming into contact every day with people who could refer you, but they don't even think about it, because you have not been prepared. You weren't dressed right, you didn't have a phenomenal message, and you didn't look for ways to help them. Now, that will all change, right? The faster you change that, the faster you'll see the cash coming in.

## FASTEST WAY TO THE CASH #13:
### Network Like Crazy!

Most small businesses are built by the owner getting out and talking to people. The problem is that most business owners aren't very good at networking. They don't come across as very professional and make many mistakes. Further, they don't intentionally expand their network of contacts. To get more cash coming in now, strategically build win-win relationships with as many people you can.

How does this bring in fast cash? When you have a phenomenal message and you get good at building relationships, you can

**When you have a phenomenal message and you get good at building relationships, you can easily connect with lots of people who can use your service or refer you right away.**

easily connect with lots of people who can use your service or refer you right away.

You can start right now. Just start contacting your social media contacts, friends, family and anyone you have in your contacts and strike up a conversation about what you're doing right now. Find ways to help them. Let them know you want to find some ways you can help each other. Any professional worth their salt will want to brainstorm if you come across professionally.

## FASTEST WAY TO THE CASH #14:
## Implement the Direct Selling Process

Follow the steps shared earlier in this book. Simply call on potential prospects and referral sources with the Secret Weapon, your phenomenal message, your Free Trial Offer, your Referral Reward Program, and your phenomenal relationship-building skills. The more calls you make, the more money you make. The faster you make the calls, the faster you get cash. Simple as that.

## In Closing...

As you can see, the fourteen fastest ways to the cash are not secretive or complicated. They are simple to do. But as the late Jim Rohn said, "Simple things are easy to do, but they are also easy 'not' to do."

I hope this book has given you a good foundation in small business marketing and reminded you of the simple steps that when implemented will help you put more CASH in your bank account.

If you find yourself not implementing these things consistently, you're not alone. Many small business owners suffer from what I call F.T.I. (Failure To Implement). F.T.I. occurs even when you know what to do! The key to phenomenal success in business is to determine why you don't implement.

Continue that search by getting someone to help you implement. Everyone needs support, encouragement, and accountability to become all they want to be. If you like what you've read and you want to go deeper and avoid F.T.I., get in touch with me to see how we can help.

Get free resources and find out about our phenomenal community that will support you, encourage you, and hold you accountable to the things YOU  want to accomplish at www.HowardPartridge.com.

Take care.

# ABOUT HOWARD PARTRIDGE

Originally from Mobile, Alabama, Howard grew up on welfare. At the age of eighteen he took a Greyhound bus to Houston, Texas, where he arrived with 25 cents in his pocket. After five years as a waiter, he started his first business out of the trunk of his car.

In 1998, he started Phenomenal Products, a training company that offers information products, training, coaching, and consulting for small businesses around the world.

Howard has been recognized by some of the world's top business authors, including John Maxwell and Michael Gerber, is the exclusive business coach for the Zig Ziglar Corporation and has been recommended by many of America's most successful marketing authors and consultants.

He is the author of three Amazon.com best-selling books: *7 Secrets of a Phenomenal L.I.F.E.*, *The 5 Secrets of a Phenomenal Business*, and *Think and Be Phenomenal—The 5 Levels of Being Phenomenal*.

Howard has been married to Denise for over 30 years, and they have one son, Christian.

Get *free* business-building resources at
www.HowardPartridge.com